# Levi's Legacy

## Jami Guinn

Library of Congress Control Number:  2004096380

  Guinn, Jami (Jami Guinn)
    [Levi's Legacy]

ISBN 0-9760802-0-6

# Introduction

In mid March of 2001 our family took food to a blind man. The next day Levi (our 4 year old) started saying he couldn't see. Naturally we thought it was just a game to him. He was not playing...within a week we found ourselves in the emergency room waiting for CT scan results. On March 23rd 2001 Levi was diagnosed with a brain stem glioma, an inoperable tumor. The life expectancy was 6 months to a year. There are countless stories of such tragedies in our world. This is ours...

I started writing updates on the website created for that purpose (www.leviguinn.org) to help friends and family stay informed of what was going on with Levi's treatments and to give specific prayer requests. As time went on it became "therapy" for me. I could write out my heart, read it... see it... and combat my fear, anger and lack of understanding with Gods word, His promises. You will notice that most of my journal entries start with me being afraid, sad, angry, overwhelmed... but end with hope for the moment. I am not a theologian. I am not a great writer... I am a brokenhearted mother who just happened to keep a record of a loving God in action.

My prayer is that somehow you, the (God-ordained) reader of this book will learn something of the character of Christ that you didn't know before... that you will "enter into" my journey, travel down this oh-so-difficult road and experience the lover of your soul pouring Himself out on you as He has me... *I pray also that the eyes of your heart may be enlightened in order that you may know the hope to which he has called you, the riches of his glorious inheritance and his incomparably great power for us who believe.* Ephesians 1:18 & 19

~jami~

# Levi's Legacy

**Saturday, April 7, 2001** *(Ed.: This and a few other updates were written by Jami's husband, Jeff)*

Levi was diagnosed with an inoperable brain stem glioma two weeks ago. We are getting through our state of shock as our lives have been rudely interrupted (from our earthly perspective). What would we do if we didn't have our Lord Jesus Christ, and our Father to bring us through this? Now that we're facing the reality of it we must make some very big decisions concerning the treatment.

After 4 days of radiation (traumatic, we might add), the Lord has made it perfectly clear that radiation and chemotherapy are not the road He would have us take. The negative effects radiation and chemotherapy have on a child (from some of our research), is more than we are willing to chance—blindness, hearing loss, borderline retardation, 4 points IQ loss per year, and the list goes on. We are now in a 2 week waiting period for getting another MRI, which is the necessary amount of time after radiation treatment. We will then send copies of the MRI to Stanislaw R. Burzynski, MD, PhD at the Burzynski Research Institute Clinic in Houston, Texas. He has developed a far safer, more effective treatment than anything traditional medicine has to offer, using "antineoplastons" (for more information go to: www.cancermed.com). He will determine if we can be immediately admitted or have to wait 8 more weeks in compliance with FDA regulations. Please pray for this specifically as time is crucial.

If so, we will be going to Houston as a family for 2-3 weeks to begin treatment. Our health insurance will not cover any of this to our knowledge and it will be incredibly expensive. After this we will return and Levi will continue treatments at home. He will have to go back to Houston every 6 weeks to see if his tumor has decreased in size.

Presently this is our plan; it may change completely. The Lord may fully heal him in the next 2 weeks just in time for his next MRI.

Elders and intercessors have prayed over him and anointed him with oil, according to James 5:13-16. Prayer is going up everywhere for our precious son. *"The eyes of the Lord are over the righteous, and His ears are open to their cry"*. Though Levi's chances for survival are very small, our *"God is able to do exceedingly above all that we ask or think, according to the power that worketh in us"*. No matter what happens, may God be glorified. Remember, GOD IS GOOD ALL THE TIME!

## Saturday, April 21, 2001

Filling in the gaps: Well, it has been just over 2 weeks now since the Lord directed us to stop Levi's radiation treatments, as the previous update below touched on. Here's how we heard from Him to change our thinking and make this difficult decision:

After a few days of strongly resisting any ideas about "alternative treatments", I was pouring my heart out to the Lord late at night on the day of the third (traumatic) treatment, asking God for clear direction and an end to confusion, when the phone rang. I let it ring and kept praying. It stopped ringing. In a moment or two, it rang again, and I felt like the Lord was saying, "answer it Jeff!". So I did. It was the grandmother of a child with exactly the same kind of tumor calling from Cincinnati. Over the next half hour or so she told me all about their experiences with traditional and alternative methods, and how successful the treatments administered by Dr. Burzynski had been. Because of the incredible timing of this call, Jami and I were beginning to reexamine our stand, but the clincher came the next morning on our way home from the fourth radiation treatment.

The three of us were sitting at IHOP finishing our breakfast, when two kind people came up to us and just started sharing from their hearts about how God created our bodies to heal themselves. The woman spoke about how her child had many difficulties growing up and how she had turned down the conventional methods in favor of natural alternatives – successfully. She spoke about radiation and chemotherapy, and the destructive effects they have on the body, especially children. Jami and I just looked at each other wondering what this conversation was all about. We had not yet even mentioned that Levi had an inoperable brain tumor. After we spoke about Levi's situation and our open hearts to whatever the Lord wanted for him, the man began to speak about a doctor that has had great success with brain tumors. He was writing down his name for us to check into, and it was the very doctor we had been researching as an alternative the last few days – Dr. Burzynski at the Burzynski Research Institute in Houston. We were really stunned, because that morning Jami and I held hands and prayed fervently that God would give us an "idiot-proof" sign of His leading ("Lord, do you want us to stop the radiation and do something else? Give us a sign today of the route You want us to take"). God sent us two angels to reveal his will for us. It sure seemed idiot-proof to us.

Levi's current condition: During these two weeks of waiting (for the next MRI), Levi has been swelling up before our eyes because of the steroids he's taking to keep the swelling of the tumor down. His appetite is very large now; he wants to eat all the time. His face is rounder and his belly looks as if it's holding a soccer ball. He has mood swings – cheerful, then maybe grumpy. Lately he has been lethargic and not too much energy. We have been giving him organic carrot/apple juice (using a juicing machine), along with immunity boosters (natural foods, herbs, etc.).

The latest additional treatment: Last Sunday night I spoke to an old friend of the family in Florida who for many years, has been plugged into a network of people around the country bent on a relentless pursuit of unbiased, truthful information about cures for this dread disease. Acting on his suggestion, Jami took Levi and drove to Columbia, SC first thing Monday morning, to meet with a scientist who has been researching cancer treatments for 25 years. He gave Levi a strict diet of "optimizers", which boost the immunity system to fight against the tumor. So this regimen will be a good supplement along with the treatment he will be getting in Houston.

The latest MRI update: We went in to Egleston Children's Hospital for the scheduled MRI Thursday at 7am...

# Levi's Legacy

We were then told that the MRI machine had just "gone down". The engineers were an hour away, but they were still not sure that it would come back up soon. We didn't want to take the chance to wait, so we rescheduled. When we got home we got a call from Dr. Soapes, our pediatrician. We told her that the MRI machine was down. She was calling to tell us that, due to a miscommunication, we were not pre-certified – which meant we would have had to pay for the MRI out of pocket. So we praised God together as we realized that God had a good reason for causing the MRI not to work. The MRI has been rescheduled for Tuesday, April 24, at 1:00 at Scottish Rite Children's Hospital, where our insurance carrier covers us.

So we are still waiting to see if the brain tumor has decreased or increased in size. When we find out Tuesday, we will quickly update you as to what our next move will be.

I am amazed at the love that has come our way from family, friends and even strangers. Meals have been coming every night for 3 weeks now. Many dear people continue to offer help, but so far every practical need has been met. People have been so generous in supporting Levi prayerfully (i.e. a couple weeks ago, a good friend of ours, Shannon, fasted from Sunday through Tuesday and met us at the hospital to pray over Levi. He came up from Columbus, Georgia – 2 hours away). Financially, many have given sacrificially to help us with Levi's treatments – our 12 year old niece, Nicole, emptied her "piggy bank" and gave us $40. It reminded me of the widow that had 2 "pennies" and gave it all. Jesus smiled on that. We are so grateful.

What we are going through is a tragedy, but an honor at the same time. Through our darkest times, the Lord is present still and very close. When everything seems good – no problems – we tend to drift from the Lord. This trial has many questions that arise, but it brings us closer to the One who we belong to. We do pray that God would be glorified in whatever happens. But we do cry out "Please heal Levi, Lord!"

Please pray for:

1. Jami's strength and rest; she needs a break somehow, restoration
2. Family unity; we feel so scattered and losing intimacy with each other / kids also
3. Jeff – self-employed, would not get overwhelmed with work and all responsibilities
4. Levi's full whole body healing, and restoration (miracle)Wednesday, April 25, 2001

## Wednesday, April 25, 2001

(3 PM) The follow-up MRI took place yesterday afternoon. The results from that have been forwarded to Dr Burzynski in Houston. Decisions and plans are being made as you read this. Please check back later for a more detailed update.

## Thursday, April 26, 2001

As you all know we had the MRI done on Tuesday. The tumor is exactly the same size. Praise the Lord for that!! The FDA requires us to wait 6 more weeks before we begin treatment in Houston. We could have begun treatment immediately if the tumor had grown. So, for now we will be going to Columbia today (April 26). We will only be there today and tomorrow. I (Jami) will probably go back next week and possibly stay for the full week next week. The Dr. wants Levi to stay there as long as possible for the treatment that they can only give him there. That's a bummer because I'll really miss the rest of my family. Thank you so much for your incredible prayer support, meals and continuous love. We are blessed. We'll keep you posted.

**Sunday, May 6, 2001**

Well, it's been about 2 weeks since our last update. I'm sorry it has taken so long to write this up. I wish I had some incredible news that Levi is completely normal and all the symptoms are gone. But that's not the case. However, we have noticed that his eyes have started to uncross just a little bit. That's really encouraging!!!!!!! Other than that not much has changed with his little (but getting bigger) body. Since I don't have a lot to tell in that area, I'll share a little about how we're doing on a daily basis:

Jeff is working a lot while Levi, Graci and I are in Columbia. Last Monday he left the house at about 8:30 am, worked until 6:00 pm so he could go to Jonah's baseball game then the boys went home with my mom and dad, so Jeff could go back to work. He didn't get home until midnight and was back out at 6:00 am the next morning to do the same thing the next day – but it was Caleb's game this time. Hopefully, this week things at work won't be so hectic.

Caleb and Jonah are going through a time of frustration right now. They are both needing individual time with us. Before the diagnosis they would get a "night alone" once a month. Jeff would take one of them out and just hang out with him, while the other one would get to hang out with me at home, we'd get the little ones to bed and play games or rent a movie or whatever they wanted to do. They really cherished those times. It's really difficult to work that out now. The most common comment from Caleb these days is "Mom, I just need to be alone." While Jonah says, "Mom, Caleb never wants to play with me anymore."

Graci and Levi are with me basically 24/7. While we're in Columbia we stay with our great friends Bill and Debby Jones and their 4 really cool kids. They have totally blessed us with their kindness and love. When we're home Graci and Levi ask when do we get to go back to Uncle Bill and Aunt Debby's. That's a special gift from the Lord.

I am doing fairly well, I just feel pulled in a million directions. Life must go on and I must do what I need to do, though I'd rather stay home and be a normal family – but that's not an option right now. I hate leaving Jeff, Caleb and Jonah for so long. I miss them terribly, and long for the day we can all be together and stay together. I'm also struggling with the changes in Levi. He's grown so much he doesn't even look the same. He's so precious but he's definitely different. Sometimes I feel like I'm grieving the loss of Levi but I can't really do that because I have a new son. I know that's weird but that's the only way I can describe how I feel. As you can tell I'm starting to get tired of this. Every time I think I've got a grip on this I'm slapped in the face with a new emotion to deal with. I have an incredible urge to go into the corner and suck my thumb these days. ha ha ha. I am clinging more than ever to the fact that my heavenly Father is two things. #1 He is sovereign, he is still in full control. "Though I stand on the Rock and tremble the Rock will not shake beneath me." And #2 He is good.

I have days when I feel strong. I feel like I can face it all. But then I have weak days. Days when I'm afraid to get up in the morning because life is hard. But the good news is in

2 Corinthians 12:9&10 ...

*"My grace is sufficient for you, for my power is made perfect in weakness. Therefore I will boast all the more gladly about my weaknesses, so that Christ's power may rest on me. That is why, for Christ's sake, I delight in weaknesses, in insults, in hardships, in persecutions, in difficulties. For when I am weak, then I am strong."*

I know this is a contrast to my last letter. I was feeling strong and ready to face the daily aspect of this journey. Today I feel afraid and weary. The warrior is really a child but my Father holds me close.

~jami~

**Wednesday, May 16, 2001**

Once again there's not much change in the medical aspect of our journey. We're still waiting for the next MRI which is at the beginning of June. After that we'll be able to see which way to go, stay in Columbia or go to Houston. If the tumor is bigger it's Houston, if the tumor is smaller we stay in Columbia.

Even though there's not much going on medically, there's a lot going on in our hearts. As I was having my quiet time this morning the Lord was really showing me His mercy... I was thinking about our whole battle with this tumor and remembering what life was like "before" it all came about. I was wondering what we would be doing if this had never happened. I'll tell you exactly what we'd be doing——The same old thing. Here's where God's mercy comes in. He knew us and how we're prone to wander away from him. Not necessarily falling into great sin but worse, walking past the Almighty without marvel and wonder. Now we see what was always true. We are completely dependent on our God. Always! We thought there was some promise that tomorrow would come just the way we would like it and the prosperity and health would continue as we planned and felt we deserved. He has been merciful to show us this. It's as if I've waited my whole life to see Him in this way. My favorite book/movie is The Hiding Place. It's a true story about Corrie Ten Boom and how she and her whole family were put into a concentration camp for hiding jews in their house... Corrie was holding her dying sister, Betsy, in her arms and Betsy looked up at Corrie and said, "When we get out of here we must tell everyone that there is no hole so deep that the hand of God cannot reach us and they will believe us because we've been here." I love that and I am so grateful that the Lord has put us in a position to testify to the length, depth and width of His love and mercy.

Also, I've been wondering how the little ones perceived God in this... Yesterday I was driving home from the grocery store. Levi and Graci were in the back seat, we were listening to praise music. There was a song that said praise the King for he is worthy. I just happened to look in the rear view mirror and saw four tiny hands raised up in the air. They were singing along with the music. Then, Levi said, "Jesus is the King." Is there any greater joy!!!!!!!!!!!!

In His mercy,

~jami~

**Wednesday, May 24, 2001**

I'm walking out the door right now to take Levi to the Dr. He has been running a fever for the last 3 days. At night it gets up as high as 103. He has been really tired and fussy. Please pray for him. I'll tell you more as I know it.

Thank you,

~jami~

**Wednesday, May 26, 2001**

Thank you for praying. In our last update we were going to the Dr. because Levi had been running a fever. I was really nervous about it. It turns out that he probably just has some kind of virus that's going around. His blood count was good and strong. (Thank you Lord) Our next prayer is that the MRI will show the tumor to be smaller or even better, gone! Wouldn't that be COOL!!?!!! The MRI is on June 4th at 10:00 am. Until then, we're going to have some fun! We're going to Disney World Monday. The Make-A-Wish Foundation has planned it all for us. A Limo picks us up at our door and takes us to the airport. (smile) We'll be there for a week. We're all so excited. Every time we get in the car Levi says, "Are we going to Disney World now?" Then, when we show up at the grocery store he starts to cry from disappointment. I can't wait to get in the limo and say NOW we're going to Disney World. Please pray that Levi would be comfortable in the heat and his little secret dreams that he can't verbalize would come true. We'll be staying at a place called "Give A Kid The World". It's a special place made especially for Make-A-Wish kids. From what I hear it's awesome. We'll take lots of pictures!

Now, could I make a request? It's pretty selfish but I'm gonna ask it anyway. I need extra prayer. Even though I'm really excited about the trip, it's hard for me to go. When I think of "Make-A-Wish" I think of kids that have little time alive and they have a wish granted before they die. Even though I try to live in the "he's going to be fine" mode I can't help but wander over into the "these are our last days with him on earth" mode. Everyone always says, "Don't think like that, he's gonna be fine." But that's (a well intended) promise that can't be made. I feel like I have to face the possibilities. In all this I still feel surrounded by the Lord and His love and mercy. But I'm still in the deepest valley of my life. I still look at him as if it's the last time I'll see him breathing. I still wonder how much time we have, I still long for him to be the way he used to be. I still feel the pressure to remember every moment and not forget it. I'm afraid I'll forget something and when it's too late I'll wish for the day when creating memories was an option. And then after I have that rush of feelings I feel guilty for not living in today more. My prayer is that we would be able to laugh, have fun... be free to live. I hope that little peek into the corner of my heart wasn't too much.

There's a song by Bebo Norman, it says ...Lord, you unfold me but then you hold me... I am truly unfolded but He is holding me.

Thank you all for your unending support and love. We are blessed beyond measure every day by prayers, e-mails, cards, letters, phone calls, gifts, meals... How could we ever show you how deeply we need all of you and how much we appreciate everything that you do for us. You are the rose among the thorns for us. May God bless you 10 fold.

We love you,

~jami~

### Tuesday, June 5, 2001

We're home! We had a great time but are very glad to be back. It was an action packed week. We went to the Magic Kingdom, Animal Kingdom, MGM, Sea World, Universal Studios (Islands of Adventure) and downtown Disney. Needless to say we're exhausted!!!!

I tried desperately to let everything go and forget "things" for one week. But all the families that stayed there had terminally ill children (some were healed and some were preparing to die). I felt a rapport with each mother, even if I never even talked to them. Since it was a vacation atmosphere most were laughing and playing with their family. But I knew that when it was quiet and their family was sleeping they were racked with pain like me. I couldn't help but feel each mothers pain.

Well, the long awaited MRI was yesterday. I didn't realize how stressed I was about it until Jan (our Dr) told us that it is SMALLER. My body went limp with relief. It's not a whole lot smaller but smaller just the same. (I love that word, "smaller"). That means we won't be going to Houston for now, we'll be going back and forth to South Carolina. We feel so blessed and taken care of by the Lord. I know there's a long road ahead of us but this is a morsel of much needed hope. This morning I read Psalms 30:11&12... *"You turned my wailing into dancing: you removed my sackcloth and clothed me with joy, that my heart may sing to you and not be silent. O Lord my God, I will give you thanks forever."* Through it all He has clothed us in joy despite the circumstances but it's so much more today. smile. I remember reading Psalms 57:1 in the "beginning" *"Have mercy on me O*

*God have mercy on me. For in you my soul takes refuge. I will take refuge in the shadow of your wings until the disaster has passed."* I know there's more to endure, however, I feel like I can peek my head out and see the sunlight.

Praise the Lord with us!!!

Our next move is trying to be normal (not that we ever were actually normal) ha ha ha. Caleb and Jonah start their All-Star practices next week. We also are praying abut next school year. Since we don't know what the future holds for Levi's treatment we're thinking it would be a good idea to get Caleb and Jonah into a Christian school. Homeschooling through this has been impossible and I have had to totally depend on my friends Cindee, Staley and my Mom. I don't know what I would have done without their help. So, now the search is on for a Christian school that we can afford and is close by. Please pray for wisdom in this area. We really need it.

Levi is doing great! His symptoms are the same. He is still a little chubster and his eyes are slightly crossed. Yesterday, he did great with his MRI. He used to cry and go crazy when they took his blood pressure and did the pulse ox and needless to say the IV was a nightmare. But yesterday he didn't even balk at it. He cried a tiny bit with the IV but what a long way he's come. He is now a 30 year old in a 4 year old's body. He's incredible. Caleb, Jonah and Graci are so excited about the shrinking tumor!! HOPE. What a beautiful thing.!!

We love you all and will keep you posted!

~jami~


## June 15, 2001

It's been two months and three weeks (84 days) since the diagnosis. This morning I was remembering the feelings I had the moment they told us and the first 2 weeks of trying to let it "soak in". Back then, I wondered what life would be like in 3 months since the doctors told us that without chemo and radiation he would have only 4 to 6 months to live. When I asked, what would happen to him through time without their treatment they said he would be blind and possibly deaf and possibly unable to walk... I, unwisely, let my imagination take me there. I was devastated to say the least. I remember asking the Lord to allow us to testify to His faithfulness whether it be healing Levi or walking with us through his death. Of course, all the while praying with every fiber in me it would be healing. So, when the report came back that the tumor was smaller... RELIEF...

Now, it's been eleven days since the "good report". For some reason I expected life to be easy after that. What was I thinking? Now, there's a new twist in daily life. (I feel ashamed to talk about it because I should be so eternally grateful that HE shrunk the tumor. I should be singing HIS praises all day long, not complaining about how difficult things are right now. But, if there's one thing I've learned about the character of God it's that He can handle the transparencies of my heart no matter how ugly they may be, and loves me anyway.)

# Levi's Legacy

The main thing I'm struggling with right now is the "everydayness" of it. Giving medicine 3 times a day (which takes about 35 minutes) and trying to be normal. All the while dealing with the psychological struggles of all the other children. The whole time I've been thinking, "wow they've really done well with this." But I didn't see the secret places of their hearts. With Levi getting all this attention they have really felt jealous but afraid to tell us because they felt so guilty for feeling that way. So, now I'm trying to regain some balance. It's been harder than I thought it would be. If I correct Levi even for the smallest thing he cries and says, "you're mad at me"... If I "let things go" a little, the other kids look at me like "what's up with that?" While we were on vacation Caleb said "It's like you're not my mom anymore, all you care about is Levi." OUCH!!!!! I don't know how I expected the rest of the kids to deal with it, but I didn't expect this. Now, I find myself crying out to the Father for help through each minute in a new a way. At night when I go to bed I am absolutely exhausted from the mental anguishes of the day. I knew it would be difficult but I never estimated this aspect into the process. As a very wise man (my daddy) once told me, "You gotta keep dancin' and it's gonna be a long song." So, I'm dancin' but I don't know how to dance to this song. I know that the same God that is healing Levi's tumor can heal the broken hearts of our other children. Please pray that God would grant us the wisdom of Solomon to deal with the struggles that come with each day.

*"He is my Lord; apart from Him I have no good thing... He has assigned me my portion and my cup. He has made my lot secure. The boundary lines have fallen for me in pleasant places; surely I have a delightful inheritance. I will praise the Lord, who counsels me; even at night my heart instructs me. I have set the Lord always before me; Because He is at my right hand. I will not be shaken. Therefore, my heart is glad and my tongue rejoices; my body also will rest secure, because He will not abandon me..."* — Psalm 16:2, 5-10

~jami~

## June 22, 2001

Things are wonderful with Levi. He is full of energy, his mind is sharper than ever, and feeling great. We are so grateful for the healing of the Lord's hand on him. Right now our faith is strong, because we have seen Him work in such a mighty way. We continue to pray for Levi's complete healing.

Levi is doing great yes, however, Jonah is going through an emotional struggle right now. He has all-star practice every night. He is a great player and normally really enjoys playing but all of a sudden he can't leave my side. I have to be where he can see me at all times or he will cry and get a tummy ache. He is constantly afraid I am going to leave him. Last night at a scrimmage game it was thundering. I looked over and he was crying. He has never been afraid of thunder before but this time he was mortified. I went into the dugout and held him. I whispered into his ear, "do you want me to pray now"? He said yes so I started to thank God for His deep love for Jonah. I quoted scripture that I thought would encourage Jonah to trust the Lord to take care of him. He was encouraged and finished the game beautifully but I was more encouraged. It was so cool to "go over" in my mind (as I was praying in Jonah's ear) the wonderful plans the Lord has for us. It's all basic stuff. But how incredible it is that God cares for us in all situations. Even in a stinky old dugout He meets us there. He is our Saviour in all situations. In the most unlikely of places He makes the ground holy ground because He is there. In our hearts we can bow down and worship Him anywhere. And we did. He is High and exalted and worthy of praise. He is Holy but approachable. He is without blemish but loves and accepts the ugly and imperfect (us). He is our refuge. The shadow in which we hide when we are afraid. The arm we "snuggle" under when we need comfort.

I have learned in my 9 plus years as a parent that there are intermittent "windows of opportunity" to make a memory of life changing proportion in the hearts of our children. I pray that last night in that dugout Jonah had one of those moments. I pray that He will never forget how deep and wide and long the love of Christ is for him because he felt His presence at his 7 year old all star practice game. I'm not sure what is going on in Jonah's little heart and mind but the "lover of his soul" does and is there to help him in a way that Jeff and I can't.

We left the game and he was happy, running, playing, singing in the car and saying, "I love you mom, I love you so much". I am encouraged. I hope you are too.

We love you all,

~jeff and jami~


**June 28, 2001**

The Lord is still being merciful to us. He has not stopped the healing process in Levi. He gets better and better every day. He has lost 6 pounds from the 10 pounds he gained from the steroids. After he was diagnosed he eerily started to ask questions about cemeteries over time as we would pass one on the road. I couldn't help but wonder what that "meant". Last night he was asking somewhere around a million questions about birth. He wanted to know everything about when he was born: "Did it hurt you so bad Mom?" "Were you glad to see me?" "Did you hold me when you saw me?" He was somewhat of an emergency C-section and was whisked away to ICU when he was born so when I told him that I kissed him and then the nurses took him away, he said, "Why did they take me away from you when you're my mommy?" It was so fun to talk about birth and life instead of death.

Since the obvious healing in Levi's body I have been able to "breathe". However, I kinda liked "suffocating" in my need for the Lord. Nicole Nordeman sings a song that I relate to...

Rolling river, (God)... little stones are smooth only after water passes through so I am a stone rough and grainy still, trying to reconcile this river's chill... but when I close my eyes and feel you rushing by I know that time brings change and change takes time and when the sunset comes my prayer would be just one... that you might pick me up and notice that I am just a little smoother in your hand ...the river sometimes raging wild, sometimes swollen high, but never have I known this river dry... the deepest part of you (Lord) is where I want to stay and feel the sharpest edges washed away...

It is our deep desire that HE would continue to smooth away the roughest edges of our hearts. So, my prayer is that in this calloused, unbelieving world we would not fall to apathy and mediocrity. This is a struggle when not "under the gun" of desperation. I know it sounds ridiculous that I would worry about falling away when for the last 3 months I have been watching God's hand heal my son. But I know me and I get busy with the daily grind, and rush by HIM, and I am ashamed to say that I feel a special bond with the Israelites when they saw the Red Sea parted, were given manna from heaven, water from rocks... and still lived as if they had never seen God's hand work. I am afraid of that part of me and find myself begging for His fire in my heart to forever burn. I'm not saying that I have forgotten Him. What I'm saying is I know my flesh and its unwillingness to die easily. My sister (Lori) gave me a quote that goes like this..."The more you sweat during peace times the less you bleed during war times." It seems to be a time of peace right now, but the war time is coming so I'm "sweating" in prayer and and hiding His word in my heart so I might not sin against Him in the "war times".

We're excited about seeing HIM glorified at Bebo and Allen's concert on the 13th of this month. Pray with us that as God heals Levi He would use this time to heal hearts and draw the lost to Him by His kindness. May we be clean vessels to carry His message of Love to the world around us.

Once again, we want you to know how much we love and appreciate you. Every e-mail, every gift, every letter, every phone call , every prayer lifted up in your closet. We are wide eyed and in awe at the Love that is being poured out on us

~jeff and jami~

## July 2, 2001

It's 11:30 at night. Everyone is sleeping. I was just thinking how the Lord gave me a gift tonight that most people might not appreciate as much as I do. Tonight, I had a "NORMAL" thing happen. Levi wanted to sleep in his room tonight. He hasn't done that since he was diagnosed. I walked him up to his room, (just like I used to). I tucked him in and we prayed together, (just like we used to). I started to walk out of the room, (just like I used to). He said, "Mom, will you sing some songs?" (Just like he used to). One thing was different. ~ ME! ~ I used to hate when he asked me to sing. That may seem harsh but since I have 4 to tuck in, pray for, love on and talk to about the issues of the day... extra curricular night time activity is not good. Especially with Levi. He would hold his chubby finger up in front of his face and say just one song mom. So, I would sing one song. Then I would start to leave the room and he would start to cry and say noooo, that wasn't the song I wanted. So, I would sing another song. Again, it wasn't the song he wanted to hear... It took around 45 minutes and 10 songs to get him to sleep. When he was sick, I would have given just about anything to hear him say, "mom, will you sing just one song?" It's been a long time, but tonight, June

30, 2001 I heard those words I longed to hear again. It was BEAUTIFUL... I would have sung to him all night long but he fell asleep after only 2 songs. ~ ~ Lord, help me to appreciate the little everyday things more. I know (now) that they aren't "everyday" for long.~ ~

~jami~

## July 14, 2001

Well, here I am again, I have brought myself here to this computer about 20 times in the last 2 weeks to give an update, but to no avail, I am completely speechless. I have never seen love like we have experienced. Father, somehow give me the words to express our gratefulness adequately.

My first thought is to mention everyone's name that has given so graciously their time, love and passion. But then I feel so overwhelmed I want to give up. So, I will focus on one today. The giver of all gifts, the creator of kindness, the one who has waited and still waits to bless without measure. The one who knows the depth of depravity in my heart but is still bent on giving me everything He has to give.

I keep a journal of the lives of my children. It's nothing glamorous, it's just a bunch of spiral notebooks tattered and torn dripping magic marker on the front with the words "Love Letters". One night I was crying because I just loved my children so much I didn't know what to do with it. I felt so unqualified to be trusted with the hearts and souls of these eternal beings. What if something happened to me? What if I died before they were old enough to know how much I loved them? Out of that dark night was born the book of "Love Letters" I started out with telling them how we came up with their names so that they would know that they were set apart from the beginning. God specifically gave us their names. Joshua Caleb (To enter Gods promised land because of his faithfulness) Samuel Jonah (A strong prophet and an evangelist {Jonah actually means dove}). Anna Grace (Anna (in scripture) was a woman who prayed and fasted in the temple until she died) and Grace for what God has drenched us in) They have become their names and we are eager to see how He unfolds the rest of their lives. Right now we are watching Levi become his name. David Levi (a king and a priest). We were at church having Levi dedicated when a friend (A godly woman named Jacquie Tyre) came up to us and told us that God had a "special" plan for Levi. That was nice but she went on. With deep conviction in her eyes she said, "Did you know that the two names David and Levi together mean 'to praise God with his life, To draw others to God'.

At that moment we knew there was a plan just like there is for our other children but we were thinking that it would be when they were older. The more I see God work the more I want to be right in the middle of what He is doing. Don't you? The more I look back at my life and the lives of others I see His hand not to be mistaken for coincidence or mere fate or good karma ...The Lord God Almighty is with us. Let the records show that we acknowledge the One true God, The God of the Bible, The Lord Jesus Christ to be the author of all good things. He is all that my heart can live for. As I focus on His character I become dizzy. Which way should I go to praise Him? Should I praise him for allowing us to feel his presence through our despair, I mean He promised He would always be with us, never forsaking us but He never promised us we would FEEL His presence, that's icing on the cake. Should we praise Him for keeping our hearts in pursuit of Him? Because we can receive no glory for that, we depend on Him to give us the desire to know Him. Should we praise Him for a tumor in the center of Levi's brain? Do we dare praise Him for the dread of every mother from the day a child is conceived? I do! I worship Him now because He is ever working in my heart. I praise Him because He has chosen the lowly (of which I am one) to be immersed in love and kindness. I am worthy of no such thing. I praise Him because I have had the honor of seeing Him in the faces of my friends and family.

While I was at the concert last night, drenched in His presence I was thinking, "this is the gospel" A gospel of high proportion, more real than I have ever heard or seen or felt. Saint Frances of Assisi said "Preach the gospel at all times. If necessary use words" Last night we saw it in the lives of Facing East, Allen, Bebo and Dicky We also had the privilege of hearing the best that words had to offer. A brilliant display of mental pictures that helped my feeble and inadequate mind to "see" Him in an even deeper and more personal way. The more we drink from the "bucket" of God the more we want. I left thirsty for more of Him last night. May it always be so …He has shown Himself alive, He speaks to us, He runs after us, His hands lay hold of me…

~jeff and jami~

p.s. If you missed the concert I am sooooo sorry. But if the chance ever arises again don't miss it. You'll be blessed. I promise.

## July 27, 2001

Obviously, there aren't many medical changes since my last update was about my childhood memories* instead of Levi. But actually it was a little bit about him. That whole thought about memories started because I had a few minutes to complete some thoughts. I wonder… if the smell of corn on the cob reminds me of all that wonderful time in my life, what will this hard time smell like in the years to come?

Lately, I have been going through a time of despair. I know that this should be a time of relaxing since his symptoms are not worsening. But, we went to the mountains last week and the change of scenery opened my mind up to what is really going on inside my heart. When we're home in the busy-ness of life it's easier to hide my "stuff". When I feel angry, frustrated, confused, anxious, fearful, guilty, resentful, rage, despair… I shove it back deep inside where it came from. I don't have time for them. I'm very busy trying to be normal. In the mornings I would take the (big) boys to a day camp. The drive home was about 35 minutes of solitude. I would just drive and think and cry and drive and think and cry… I had to deal with all the emotions inside… Memories. I remember my childhood and the purity of it. Then I wonder about my children and what they will remember. What will become of them?

Will they live that long? Or will I bury one of them before they have a chance to make many memories? When I watch them sleep I cry because they are so peaceful. They are so beautiful. I wonder if there is anything more wonderful than knowing that they are safe and warm and resting. Then a new thing comes into my mind. Something that I never thought of "before". The best thing about watching my children sleep is the hope that they will wake up. My mind makes me think about the possibility of them not waking... I know that's so depressing, but what can I say — that's how I think these days.

Then I make myself stop. Okay, there are hard things in life but let's focus, Jami. From whom does our hope come? Jesus. Okay. Regroup... His promises are worth lifting my head to look at. I must pick myself up by the bootstraps and praise Him. I must choose to swing the pendulum of my emotions to the side of hope rather than despair. I will sing for joy at the work of His hand. I must turn my eyes to him and let the things of this world dim in the light of His glory. Remember, He will never leave me or forsake me. His promises are eternal and cannot be taken. Even death has nothing on us. You are God, you are life and I will worship you forever. Into your hands I will commit myself, my family, my children. You knew them when they took their first breath and you know the day they will take their last. You are life. I will plant my feet on you, my Rock. Today, I choose you and your promises. But, tomorrow is coming Lord, please help me to choose you again. You know me and how I tend to concentrate on the negative. Balance me, anchor me. Just hold me.

I know that I might share too much of my heart and soul. I realize you might be thinking, "Why does she always bleed on me?" But please indulge me, it's therapeutic for me. Thanks for listening.

If you haven't noticed I love a good "quote" to sum up a thought! Well, I've been making up my own along the journey. Here's one that I really like. "Life is not about BEING the person God has called you to be. It's about BECOMING the person God has called you to be." So, bear with me... I'm know I'm far from "being" but I am busy "becoming."

~jami~


**August 1, 2001**

This past weekend we went to Birmingham to see Dicky and Betsy. Levi was not feeling well the whole weekend. The other children had had a virus (24 hour) and he had the same symptoms. But he started favoring his left side again. I hoped it was just my imagination. Sunday night he had a bad headache. He woke up several times in the night crying. Monday morning we called Jan (our Dr./friend) to schedule an MRI. She called the neurologist at Egleston and he said we needed to take him to the emergency room. My belly turned to mud and steel. It has not gone back to normal as of yet. The I.V. process was just like it was the first day. He was screaming out of control, he couldn't be reasoned with. They had to wrap him up in a sheet. It was miserable. I wondered what I would hear come from the doctor's mouth this time. The emergency CT scan was to rule out two possibilities, #1 metastasizing of the tumor, meaning, has it multiplied? or #2 has the tumor blocked the cerebral fluid which would mean he would need a shunt ( a tube that would open the flow to his brain) put in his head. The Dr. came in at about 4:30 and told us that it was neither of those things. PRAISE THE LORD! So, the final word is that it is just the virus that his body is having a hard time fighting.

My heart is still pounding from that one. The whole way to the hospital I was wondering if this was "it." I couldn't help it. I know a positive attitude would have been more desirable but I just couldn't work one up. I couldn't help but envision what it would be like to leave the hospital without him. How do you do that? The practical side of a brain tumor and the real possibility of death hit me right between the eyes. I thought I had considered all the implications. But I hadn't even scratched the surface of the torment, pain, and just plain old broken heartedness that goes with it. My cruel mind was taking me to the funeral home purchasing a casket and flowers… since we're at the 4 1/2 month mark and the doctor's said he would live 4 to 6 months it seemed "right on schedule" to have him digress. I lost so much hope during that "waiting period." I must admit that I was asking God, wouldn't it be so much better if we all just died in a car accident or something quick? Lord, I could handle it so much better if you could just take us ALL right now. I could embrace death as long as we were all together, but the thought of having to separate was so gut wrenching. I was totally unprepared for it. When my children complain about things not being fair I always say "life isn't fair, it's hard and it only gets harder as you get older, so get used to it." I usually say that half kidding, half hoping they will grasp the truth in the statement. But as we were driving to the hospital on Monday I was thinking about that and thinking life isn't only hard and unfair it's absolutely unbearable today. I'm still emotionally recovering and I'm not sure if I ever will fully.

The good news is once again the Lord was with us. We were more afraid than ever. We were forced to search even deeper for the everlasting spring of life. It wasn't a "feel good" thing. It was a desperate dig into the inner life of Christ. The "suffering along with him" part of the journey. The valley. The part you know will come in life but you hope doesn't come any time soon. The searching part. The "is my heart really a place that welcomes Him?" part. I must say that I prefer the warm fuzzy part of "the walk", the part where you go to church all dressed up and sing about His faithfulness… No, I take that back. I realize that it's the desperate moments that bring depth to the "warm fuzzy" moments. So, once again (still), we are declaring the Lords faithfulness, his gentle hand holding us along the way . His tender pull toward understanding Him in a new way. The world is growing more and more dim and I think that is the ultimate goal, isn't it?

still shaking,

~jami~

# Levi's Legacy

## August 12, 2001

It's been a while since I've updated you because we've just been so incredibly busy. I wish I could bring good news this update but it's not that great. You remember the virus that Levi had 2 weeks ago? Well, he's gotten over the virus however, he still throws up his medicine every time we give it to him. So, that means he is not getting what he needs to de-toxify his body. He is still favoring his left side, he gets really tired and is extremely emotional. I know that the Lord is not surprised by this bump in the road. There is a good reason for this. We just can't see it (yet). We are looking into a nutritionist right now. I have been cooking foods that increase the ph in the body (which is what Levi needs) but it's really hard to think up new things. The kids are soooo sick of steamed asparagus. They used to love it but 3 nights a week is a bit much I must admit.

Spirits in the house are pretty good right now. Caleb and Jonah begin school tomorrow. That will be really strange to have them gone when I'm so used to having them around all day. They are excited and very ready to go! Graci will turn 3 years old on the 17th. She acts like she's 33. What a hoot she is, she used to be such a tomboy but she is coming into such a "girly" stage. Dolls, dolls, dolls and pink, and pretty dresses. The boys think it's great!!!!! Levi, is tired a lot. But when he does have energy he is playing mommy and daddy with Graci or Superman with a towel strapped to his back. smile. He has lost (almost) all of his weight. He looks great and is so much more comfortable now. When he is feeling emotional he constantly tells me how much he loves me. He puts his chubby hand on my face and looks into my eyes and says "I love you mommy, and I like you too" It's one of those moments that I wish I could put on hold but can't. Jeff is doing well, he is planning a trip to Africa in September. He and my dad will be going on a construction trip with 3 other guys to renovate a missionary house. There will be time to witness to the villagers at night. I'm so excited for them. I hope their relationship with HIM will be forever deeper because of it. Jeff does have moments when he wants to back out of the trip because he's afraid to leave us. But, it's a chance of a lifetime!

We will be having an MRI scheduled probably next week. I'm kinda scared though. Since he hasn't been able to take his medicine I wonder what that means for the size of the tumor. Sometimes I get really tired of this whole thing. I wish I didn't have to always be afraid. Afraid that he will take a turn for the worse. Afraid that I haven't done enough to fight this. The stress level in the house has been high lately. Levi's fluctuating emotions take their toll on all of us. One minute he's laughing and the next he's crying for some unknown reason. My patience runs out often and I get onto him but then I remember (usually after I've "shown myself") the changes in his little body. Then I feel so guilty for not having more patience. I have to say "I'm sorry" to all the kids a lot lately. I've always wanted to be one of those soft-spoken, sweet spirited Christian women. You know the ones that speak softly and never raise their voice. They always seem to be thinking kind thoughts and saying kind words, constantly giving of themselves and never complaining... But I'm not!!!!!!! I'm one of those overbearing, loud women that make the sweet spirited women feel really uncomfortable. But, I'm working on letting the Lord radiate His sweetness through me. I'm praying that He will be patient through me. I'm praying that His mercy would be evident through me so that in my loud, obnoxious, mind-speaking foolishness my children will see a loving, forgiving, kind and merciful God who has incredible plans for them. Here's a great verse I pray the Lord will work in my heart to benefit those around me. (I've changed it to speak to me) *"The mouth of the righteous (woman) utters wisdom and (her) tongue speaks what is just. The law of (her) God is in (her) heart; (her) feet do not slip."* Psalm 37:30,31 Glory to Him!!

~jeff and jami~

## August 18, 2001

Yesterday was Graci's 3rd birthday. Where does the time go? She adds so much to our family. She's like the exclamation point at the end of our sentence. I will never look at my children's' birthdays the same again. He gave us another year with her and we are so grateful. Today is Caleb's football jamboree game. He loves playing and we love to see him play (of course, I cringe every time a big guy comes close to him and his skinny little body). Jonah is not playing football but enjoying watching and cheering for Caleb. The first week of school was great, both the boys LOVE their teachers, they argue over which one has the nicest teacher (I realize that will not last long). Levi is doing the same. Which is not that great. He is still favoring his left side a lot. He barely uses his left hand and even holds it up with his right hand so that it doesn't flop around. He gets very emotional at times and cries randomly. We have an MRI scheduled for the 22nd of August. If the results show that the tumor is bigger or even the same then we will be leaving for Houston, TX. Our tentative plans are to leave on the 25th. Caleb and Jonah will stay behind for school. I can't stand the thought of leaving them. Jeff will come back after 4 or 5 days and Levi, Graci and I will stay for 2 more weeks. I must say I look ahead with dread. I know God has some great plan for us. I know because He has proven Himself over and over again. But my flesh is weak and faithless. I would just prefer to stay home and do normal, everyday things. This is where the Lord has us right now and I am trying to embrace the refining process. I was talking to my brother (Dicky) last night about "the process". With everything in life the process is the most difficult. The end result is the easy part. (The only exception is eating sunflower seeds in which the process of breaking open the seed is more fun than actually eating the seed.) Smile.

In my distress I think of Isaiah 40:1, *"Comfort, comfort my people, says our God."* He continues to draw us close to Him by allowing us to go through the most difficult of times and then speaking tenderly to us, calling us to nestle in His arms. Then He pushes us out "on the limb" (again) allowing us to fail, helping us up, comforting us and then letting us try again... All this goes on and on until we get it right. Then when we get it right we find out that He did it all just to reward us in the end. The reward: A deeper knowledge and understanding of our Creator. A "romance" with Him, An eye-opening realization that life is all about investigating and uncovering the evidence of a God "in love" with His people. We are allowed to go through the valley not because God is mean but because He is good and wants desperately for us to know Him and not just a little but to the fullest.

Lord, help us to never forget. Give us the strength to carry on. Give us the wisdom to choose you, daily. As the world comes crumbling down around us please hold us up. We're so weary. Amen.

~jeff and jami~

**August 22, 2001**

Unfortunately we don't have good news this time. With a heavy heart I must tell you that, according to today's MRI report, Levi's tumor has taken on renewed vigor. The doctor says it is 20-30% larger now than compared to the original MRI back on March 23rd, even though we all know it was shrinking as of the MRI in June, as well as by all outward evidence until just a few weeks ago.

Plans are proceeding to go to the Burzynski Research Institute Clinic in Houston, Texas on Saturday where a new round of special treatments will start.

Updates will be provided as soon as we know more. Please renew your prayer efforts on Levi's behalf! And don't forget to intercede for Jeff and Jami. This is naturally a heavy blow.

Thanks so much,

Mel

**August 25, 2001**

It's early in the morning on Saturday the 25th. We'll be leaving in a few hours, if I can get it all together. Yesterday Levi had a broviac put in his chest. A broviac is a tube that goes directly into his artery so that giving him his medicine is easier. It's kinda gross looking. There's a little bloody hole in his shoulder and then out comes a tube in the center of his chest. The tube has two more tubes that fork out of the main tube and sorta "flop" around when he moves. At first he was not liking it. The whole way home from the hospital he was asking questions about his "new existence". "How will I go down the stairs now?" "How will I eat now?" Then he said, "Mom, I can't breathe, I can't breathe" in a panicked voice. (Inside I was afraid it was some strange reaction to the tube or the tumor was swelling and causing trouble for him) but on the outside I acted calm and said, yes you can, you're fine, just breathe. He relaxed and said, "Oh, okay." And he was fine. He's so funny.

Yesterday before the surgery he was with Aunt Lori all day. In the car on the way to the hospital he said, from the back seat,"God is Jesus' Father and Jesus is God's son and He's the one who is gonna heal me." I'm such a faithless dud lately, it really helps to know that he still believes. I still know the Lord is with us. I still trust His plan is perfect. However, I have allowed my mind and heart to wander ahead to the "what ifs." And if I've learned anything through this it's that you can't do that. It will paralyze you.

I find myself "making" memories. I am sometimes afraid that is all I will have soon. I have been struggling with my thoughts. I look at him sleeping and see his chest move up and down with each breath. My thought is, I should enjoy watching this, someday soon, his chest might not move up and down with life. When I touch him and his body is so warm, my thought is, soon his body might not be warm. What will I do if I touch him and his body is cold. Then I can't function the rest of the day. I just cry all day. I know these are morbid and horrible thoughts but that is where my mind has been lately. Our pain level is contingent on Levi and his symptoms. When he is somewhat "normal" we are okay. But when his symptoms worsen, we fall into desperate thoughts. The truth is that those things will happen, maybe now, maybe when Levi is 80. Only God knows. So, now, we must look to Him to get us out of the sin of "looking too far ahead" and let me tell you He knew what He was talking about when He said *"Don't worry about tomorrow, tomorrow has enough trouble of its own."* –Matthew 6:34.

TODAY Oh TODAY, what a beautiful thing. We have NOW and TODAY. That's it!! It's all we've ever had. C. S. Lewis said, "The greatest thing is to be found at one's post as a child of God, living each day as though it were our last, but planning as though our world might last a hundred years." That's a lot easier said than done. But I am asking the Lord to help me get back in step with HIM.

I imagine me and my heavenly father dancing. Our hearts are one and we are beautiful together. We move to the music perfectly, we are the music. But then let my heart wander into tomorrow, I fall to fear. The dancing, the music, the beauty… it stops. Then, I focus my thoughts on Him. His love, His mercy, His power, His goodness… Ahh, I can dance again, together our hearts are getting in step again. He was waiting on the dance floor. He was the same, He was patient. His arms were open… and today we dance, we twirl, we laugh, our hearts are becoming one again… Help me Lord to choose the comfort of your arms, the beauty of your song… A little dramatic I know but it's the picture He gave me and I like it.

Love, blessings, joy and lots of dancing to you all!!!!!!!!!!!!

~jeff and jami~


## September 7 , 2001

Hi… It's Jeff this time. Jami hasn't had access to the computer for two weeks now. She misses her early morning "ritual" of spending time working out, reading the bible, praying, and journalizing her thoughts on this here computer. I miss her…

She and I, along with Graci and Levi drove to Houston on August 25 to start treatment at Dr. Burzynski's clinic. It was the day after Levi had outpatient surgery at Scottish Rite Children's Hospital, where he had a tube implanted into his main artery near his heart. This was to ready him for immediate IV treatment of the controversial non-toxic "antineoplaston" drug.

Our first appointment with Dr. Burzynski was on Monday the 27th. Levi's treatment actually began on Tuesday and the only side effects he has had is that he is very tired and lethargic, and this was expected. The doctors have been gradually increasing the dosage volume every day so that his body can handle the "peptide fragments" circulating through his bloodstream. They want Levi to be able to attain to the 160cc dosage every 4 hours of the A10-type antineoplaston. Right now he is at 50cc.

We are staying in a hotel room (clean, safe and pleasing to Jami – there is a treadmill in the exercise room), 5 minutes from the clinic. Levi has appointments 7 days a week for about 3 weeks. The first week was very trying because our appointments would last 4-5 hours. The kids would get frustrated because they would have to stay contained with us while we were learning how to administer the IV bags, tubes, flushing, programming the pump, etc. We have learned how to do everything by ourselves now so the remaining visits should not be that difficult. They are regularly checking Levi's blood for any imbalances. We thank the Lord he doesn't have to get the "big bad NEEDLE" anymore. In the last 5 months of this trauma, getting stuck with the needle has been his main battle. What a trooper he is. You gotta meet this guy! God has blessed us with such an awesome little champ. I am so glad we brought Graci. She really keeps things lively and not so boring.

Well, I'm speaking like I'm still there, but I flew back home Sunday night, the 2nd. I have work to do and need to be with Caleb and Jonah. Jami's mom, Judy, met me at the airport in Houston to "relieve" me (tag team effort), and to help Jami with the "load". I thank God our parents are here to help us during this hardship in our lives. We honestly have so much to be grateful for. Jim (my father-in-law), watched and worked for me while I was away. Mom and Dad took the kids to school, watched them for us, and took Caleb to football practice.

Jami would like everyone to especially pray that the doctors would release Levi early; she wants to be a "real" family again. I cancelled my mission trip to Africa this morning after much prayer and counsel. Jim and I were going (he still is) to Zambia to renovate a missionary house in a small village (our part is the plumbing) on September 15. My family comes first, even above ministry – God told me so!

I will probably be flying back to Houston Wednesday the 12th(?) to drive back with the family after Levi's release.

OH! There have been many encouraging emails sent to us from old friends, new friends and even strangers. Thank you. The words that you put down are very real and meaningful to us. One specifically today blessed me from my old friends, Mike and Amy Kelly. "Our hearts ache for you but more importantly God's heart is aching for you too!" That really ministered to me this morning before I went to work. It reminded me that God is very near to us and He is hurting for us too. Thanks. I was just reading Psalm 34, and verse 18 says, *"The Lord is near to them that are of a broken heart, and saveth such as be of a contrite spirit. Many are the afflictions of the righteous: but the Lord delivers him out of them all"*. All I know is that God knows what He is doing with Levi, and we are going to trust Him no matter what happens (Isaiah 55:6-9). His ways are higher than our ways.

Jeff

## September 15 , 2001

We're Home!!!!! It was the longest 3 weeks of our lives. We started our journey home
Thursday at about 1:00 pm. We drove for about 7 hours. (Of course we didn't get as far as
we would have liked to because we had to stop so often to eat. Levi is on steroids again and
can't think about anything but food. He gained 8 pounds in 3 weeks) We finished up our
drive on Friday and got home about 3:00 pm. Jeff picked up the boys at school and killed
time so that we could get in the house and "hide". We had told Caleb and Jonah that we
wouldn't be home until Saturday. Graci, Levi and I hid behind the couch and waited until they
came in the door. We jumped out and yelled "SURPRISE!!!" It was the sweetest reunion!!!.
Jonah ran and jumped in my arms crying. Caleb just stared with his mouth hanging open.
Levi cried with open arms toward Jeff. Graci went from person to person hugging. We were
all crying. It was the most wonderful moment!!! I dreamed and cried often while in Houston
about holding my boys again. It was even better than I had imagined. We were together
FINALLY!!!!! When the attack came to America on Tuesday I had a panicked heart. I felt like I
had to get home IMMEDIATELY. It felt as if the world were crumbling around me and I
couldn't be with my family. I went to the doctors and told them that I HAD to get home!! But
they said NO. I thought I was going to explode!! I just about "lost my testimony" if you know
what I mean. I came dangerously close to complete panic!!! As it was it was only partial
panic. I had to focus on God's sovereignty. It was the most difficult time of choosing to trust
Him I have ever had. I told Him that He was pushing me way too far on this one. "How could
you Lord?" I know you are with us but you just stand by and do nothing. I'm so tired of this
Lord, I'm exhausted of this walk in the dark. Give us some light here. I can't take it
anymore!!! It took me quite a while to see. But the next morning in my time alone He gave
me enough light to get me through the day. I have prayed the prayer of Jabez even before Levi
was diagnosed: ..."Lord, enlarge my borders (my range of testifying to His faithfulness)"...
Well, He did. But here I was, standing on the edge of that border terrified at the vastness of
it. It brought me to the next part of the prayer..."let your hand be with me"... because I'm
freaking out!!! (that part isn't in the Bible but it's in my heart) I really and truly want to be
with you Lord, honoring you always, getting to know the depth of your character, trusting you
with each scary step of my new life. I have never known such dependence. I would like to say
that I peacefully and willingly surrender to His molding. But let me be painfully honest. I feel
myself kicking, screaming and crying all the way to the "anvil" I pray for the strength to
surrender to your touch of greatness. It's so much more difficult now.

I know that I am kinda rambling about the "happenings" of my heart... forgive me. Levi's
handling his new treatment pretty well. He is extremely tired and emotional. It's kinda hard
for him to get around because he's attached to an I.V. bag all day long. He is also having a
hard time getting used to his "new" body. It's much larger than it was just 3 weeks ago. He
was sitting on the potty the other day and he leaned forward, when he did his belly scraped
the toilet seat. He moaned. I said, what is it? He looked up and said. "I'm fat!" Poor little
man.

Oh! This is totally off the subject but what a sweet story of his (Levi) love and understanding
of Jesus' love for us. One day we were praying and after we said Amen, Graci said, "I don't

like Jesus" (my heart sank, but I tried to remain calm) I said, "Why not?" She said, "I just don't, I like the devil" (I was trying to understand where she was coming from, realizing that she is only 3). But right then Levi said "Grace, the devil is sooo bad, he wants to choke you till you die (a bit graphic, I know) and he wants to chase you and scare you. He wants to make it dark and scary for you. But Jesus wants to hug you and scratch your back and play puzzles with you and wrestle with you. He loves you Grace." …I didn't have to say anything, he had said it all. Graci had a new and profound understanding of Jesus and His sweetness… she said "Oh, I do love Jesus, and I don't like the devil." WHEW!!!!!! I also realized that Levi's perception of Jesus is a reflection of Jeff and how he loves on the kids. What a statement!!!!!!

God's word is GOOD…

*"You have set your glory above the heavens, From the lips of children and infants you have ordained praise because of your enemies, to silence the foe and the avenger. When I consider your heavens, the work of your fingers, the moon and the stars, which you have set in place, what is man that you are mindful of him, the son of man that you care for him?"* Psalm 8:1b-5

*"O righteous God, who searches minds and hearts bring to an end the violence of the wicked and make the righteous secure".* Psalm 7:9

I pray that in this time of fear and insecurity that you will seek the heart of your creator. I pray that you would become a more intense student of His character. There is so much change in these times we live in. It's too much for us spoiled Americans to handle. We have had such security in our lives. In the last 6 months I have learned a lot. But the most important thing I have learned is that focus is everything. If we focus on the problem we will crumble. But if we focus on Jesus and His goodness, His perfection, … We have Life and security beyond the mind's conception…

*"As for God, his way is perfect, the word of the Lord is flawless. He is a shield for all who take refuge in Him. For who is God besides the Lord? And who is the Rock except our God? It is God who arms me with strength and makes my way perfect. He makes my feet like the feet of a deer; He enables me to stand on the heights. He trains my hands for battle… You give me your shield of victory, and your right hand sustains me; you stoop down to make me great. You broaden the path beneath me, so that my ankles do not turn".* Psalm 18: 30-36

Blessings upon blessings,

~jeff and jami~


## September 19, 2001

Well, we're getting settled in and trying to get used to the extra daily activities. We have to get I.V. bags ready and change catheter tips, change the dressing on Levi's broviac (tube in his chest), give oral medicine… Sometimes it takes us over an hour just to get the I.V. bags ready. I must say it's quite comical. I'll be cooking dinner, putting football pads in, helping with homework, talking on the phone… priming I.V. bags all at the same time. It's kinda weird to have medical equipment spread out on the kitchen table while I'm doing my other daily duties. Everyone is already used to it. They all help out. They take turns flushing out Levi's tubes. It's an honored position to be able to push the syringe in. Levi has the power to choose who will be "the one." Caleb and Jonah have both asked if they can take Levi to school for show and tell. Their classes have been praying (every day) for him.

Levi is doing okay and only okay. He is so heavy right now he can hardly move. I can't tell if he's having side effects from the steroids or the tumor. I must say that I have developed a deep hatred for decadron (the steroid). I really miss his original little body. He now weighs 52 pounds when just 3 weeks ago he was only 40 pounds. He wakes up every hour and a half to go to the bathroom because of the huge amounts of fluid going into his body. So, Jeff and I rotate nights to sleep. Levi sleeps in our room on a pallet. When he wakes up to go to the bathroom we have him go in a hospital urinal because it's just easier than getting him up and into the bathroom with the I.V. bag. We thought about just letting him wear a pull-up (diaper) but he wouldn't hear of it.

Yesterday was a tearful day for me. Some days are just that way. I can't really control it. I had to go shopping for Levi some new clothes. That is always hard because when I hold the clothes up and look at them they're empty. Just clothes, with no little body in them. My mind goes… and I have to retrieve it before it goes too far… I just found out that Levi's doctor in Houston (Dr. Bestak) died of a massive heart attack on Saturday. I just saw him on Thursday. I am in shock. I also talked to a guy that we met in Houston at the clinic. His father was getting treatment for a brain tumor… he died last Monday. My heart sunk when I heard. My hope took a blow, not to mention my feeling of complete remorse for their loss. But, I must remember that my hope is not in the doctors. My hope is in Christ. So, that brings me back to the daily realization that I depend on Christ for every breath. I must admit fighting depression has been the "battle of the day" lately. I seem to be surrounded by death and impending death. I met so many people in Houston that had been given months or even weeks to live. Sorrow is something I feel every day. I used to not understand what it was. Now I know it well. But Jesus was a "man of sorrows" – He understands and calls us to seek His face in the midst of it, which is easy because where else would I go?

In Psalm 6:6,7 & 9 David wrote: *"I am worn out from groaning; all night long I flood my bed with weeping and drench my couch with tears. My eyes grow weak with sorrow… the Lord has heard my cry for mercy, the Lord accepts my prayer."*

In Psalm 5:2&3 He wrote: *"Listen to my cry for help, my King and my God, for to you I pray. In the morning, O Lord, you hear my voice; in the morning I lay my requests before you and wait in expectation."*

I know of a girl (Carole Shultis) that was very sick when she was 5 years old. She had to soak in tubs of ice water to keep her fever down. She had to get countless shots and go through things that no 5 year old should have to go through. She was not expected to live. She is now a grown woman with children of her own. She doesn't remember the physical pain she went through so long ago. She only remembers the pain and anguish she saw in her mothers eyes every time she looked at her. I am trying so hard to "cover up" the pain in my eyes when I look at Levi. But I know he sees it. Last night he was sleeping. I came in the room and just held him. I was crying and a tear fell on him. He woke up and saw me. I tried to smile and cover it up. He turned his head and wouldn't look at me. Lord, help me to be strong and joyful to keep him from any unnecessary pain.

We are so dependent on your prayers and so grateful for the commitment we feel from all of you. Please continue to bring us before HIS throne so that whatever the outcome HE would be glorified in our lives. If "life is but a vapor" Lord, let my vapor be a pleasant one to you.

~jeff and jami~

**September 21, 2001**

I just ran across this verse while having my quiet time. WOW! It's a great one for the times. It's a call to pursue The Lord and His truth. His word and His ways should be the priority of our minds and hearts.

*"Who have you so dreaded and feared that you have been false to me, and have neither remembered me nor pondered this in your hearts? Is it not because I have long been silent that you do not fear me? I will expose your righteousness and your works, and they will not benefit you. When you cry out for help let your collection of idols* (house, jobs, image…anything that is more important to us than HIM) *save you! The wind will carry all of them off, a mere breath will blow them away. BUT THE MAN WHO MAKES ME HIS REFUGE WILL INHERIT THE LAND AND POSSESS MY HOLY MOUNTAIN."* Isaiah 57:11-13)

Oh Lord, this is my prayer to you, to seek your face and worship you forever that I may know you in the secret place and dwell with you forever. Oh bless us Lord. Put in our hearts a desire to know you and to the fullest. Lord help us in our foolishness to fear you and tremble at your holiness. You have an inheritance for those who do. You have mercy for those who open their hearts to you. You have kindness and peace as a gift for those that lay bare the wickedness hidden within. Lord help us to honor you always. As a family I pray that we will not be only "patriots" for our country but faithful (whatever the cost) servants to our true King. I pray that at this time we will not point our finger of hatred at the religion of Islam but point our fingers back at ourselves. *"If my people, who are called by my name will humble themselves and pray and seek my face and turn from their wicked ways, then will I hear from heaven and will forgive their sins and will heal their land. Now my eyes will be open and my ears attentive to the prayers offered…"* 2 Chronicles 7:14 &15

We need to confess our own sins before Him. We need to concentrate on what we have done to remove the hands of protection on our country. We have (as a country) allowed abortion, homosexuality, prayerlessness… we don't even acknowledge God/Jesus. If we think we are going to build a bigger, better, stronger country than before without seeing that God is calling us to humble ourselves and see that we have walked away from our protection in Him we are fools.

I know this is a yet another radical letter but I think the times deserve a firm warning to get our own hearts in order before we head out to war. This country pride is just a ploy from the enemy (the devil that is) to keep our focus on anything but our own relationship with Jesus. Ahhhh Jesus. I'm so tired of this pluralistic god thing. Jesus is the one who brought us salvation. In Him our hope is and always will be. Everyone is so afraid to say JESUS. It makes me sick!!!!!!!! …JESUS, JESUS, JESUS, JESUS, JESUS, JESUS, JESUS, JESUS, JESUS, JESUS, JESUS, JESUS, JESUS, JESUS, JESUS, JESUS!!!!!!!!!

I hope this letter found your heart and soul open and not closed to Him and His call to stand. Because I think this will separate the "men" from the "boys".

~jami~

**September 29, 2001**

It's Saturday morning. Everyone is asleep and I am in my "quiet place." I love it here. My thoughts are clear and complete…

Things are pretty much the same with Levi. He is still very heavy and immobile. He is still obsessed with food because of the steroids. He sometimes wakes up in the middle of the night just to ask if it's almost time for breakfast. He still wakes up every hour or two to go to the bathroom. He is such a sweet little man. Last night he tried to go to the bathroom by himself so he wouldn't have to wake us up. I woke up to him crying with frustration because he couldn't do it. He has very little use of his left arm and leg and gets off balance. But what a precious angel he is to try to let us sleep.

We're in a waiting period right now. I liken it to our country. It's an anticipatory time of wondering what tomorrow will bring. Will we attack the enemy or will they attack us again? Will the tumor get bigger or will the treatment work? We're just sitting around waiting. But in this time of "holding on" Jeff and I have been "gettin' with God", enjoying His presence, staying in "The Word." If the chipmunks and squirrels know to store up food in the Summer to prepare for the Winter then shouldn't we do the same? Surely I'm smarter than a chipmunk(?) But it's not food I think we should be storing up, It's His word, His heart, His ways. *"Blessed is the man who delights himself in the law (word) of the Lord, and meditates on it day and night. He is like the tree planted by streams of water, which yields its fruit in season and whose leaf does not wither…* (Psalm 1:2&3) *"I desire to do your will, O my God; your law is within my heart."* (Psalm 40:8) *"Create in me a pure heart, O God, and renew a steadfast spirit within me."* (Psalm 51:10) *"O God, you are my God, earnestly I seek you; my soul thirsts for you, my body longs for you, in a dry and weary land where there is no water."* (Psalm 63:1) *"Find rest, O my soul, in God alone; my hope comes from Him."* (Psalm 62:5)

In reading all those scriptures you must think "Wow, she's so strong." Quite the contrary. I find myself peeking around today, looking at tomorrow afraid of it and what might come with it. That is why I so desperately cower in Gods word. I stay there absorbing all I can until I have the strength to come out and "face the day" Christ is my strength. His word is my hope. The Lord is my "calm."

Henry Drummond wrote about Christ's life (of which my life cannot be compared):

"Christ's life outwardly was one of the most troubled lives that was ever lived:

tempest and tumult, tumult and tempest, the waves breaking over it all the time.

But the inner life was a sea of glass. The great calm was always there."

In the stillness, in the time of meditating on Him, His ways, His thoughts... my conclusion is this: Life is not about avoiding the waves, the "tempest", the "tumult". No, It's about finding Him and His calm in them. Because the "storm" will come. There's no question about that. The only question is what will we do with it when it comes.

Oh Lord, do in our lives what you will. Prepare us for what lies ahead... Glory to Him who was and is and is to come.

~jeff and jami~

### October 3, 2001

We had a little "bump in the road" yesterday. Levi was having a bad headache all day. When I took him to the doctor his vital signs were bad. His blood pressure was 122/90, his respirations were 52. When Jan (doctor/friend) checked his eyes she could tell that there was pressure in his brain. So, we went to the hospital to get an emergency CT scan and an X-ray. Jan and I were thinking that maybe I had come down on the steroids a little too quickly and it was causing this reaction. He also has a cold so the combination could cause swelling in his brain. I was really nervous because he was drooling and slurring his words, he was falling a lot and his left hand was hurting now because it was drawing up so tight. But the CT scan didn't show any acute change, the chest X-ray was good and the blood work was normal. What a relief! So, now we're just working on getting rid of the cold and we'll have to up the steroids again. We'll schedule the MRI a little earlier than originally planned. So, it will probably be sometime next week. ...yesterday constituted a bad day...

But, the really cool thing was this: before any of this happened yesterday I called my Mom and asked if she could come help me because I felt overwhelmed with it all. She came over right away (I have an awesome Mom) and hung out with the kids so that I could workout (relieve stress). When I run I listen to praise music so that I can "focus" on eternal things. Well, it was the best run I've had in a long time. But more importantly it was a great time with Jesus. He clarified some things I had been praying for guidance on and he just loved on me. I felt like He was preparing me for something. I even thought "Wow, I wonder what is going to happen soon that the Lord is giving me such a huge measure of faith and comfort?" I was totally overwhelmed with the knowledge that He is in control and that His ways are good and with purpose. I was thinking, after my time with Him...

1. How addicted I am to His word; He gives me a "high" (something that gives such pleasure is usually sinful in our worldly ways, but not Him, He gives a pure and clean pleasure with no guilt).

2. How I depend on Him to get me through the day and He is never intimidated by the depth, width and length of my cavern of need.

3. How I get up in the morning in great anticipation to what He will be talking to me about that day

4. I am a willing prisoner to His Love, His bondservant (yet I've never been more free); like the woman at the well, He confronts me with the sins of my heart but loves me anyway and even gives me honor and dignity in His confrontation; His ways are gentle and kind, not harsh and hateful as the world thinks.

5. Where would we be without Him? Nothing could ever compare to the promises we have in Him. *"My soul will be satisfied as with the richest of foods; with singing lips my mouth will praise you"* (Psalm 63:5).

6. His desire, in our "storm" is to sanctify us, not to sink us.

7. In the last 6 months we have learned this to be true:"Jesus is all we have, He is all we need and all we want. We are shipwrecked on God and stranded on His omnipotence." (Vance Havner)

I know this was just a blob of unorganized thoughts but I hope somewhere in there you were blessed by His ways. It was my intent to give you a little glimpse of how He "is" in dark valleys. So that if you are ever afraid of the valleys that lay ahead, afraid that you couldn't handle it, you will be comforted in knowing that He is handling it. He has not left us or forsaken us. He has blessed us. He is working out His perfect plan in us. He is molding us into His image. He is still good, He is helping us to see His bigger picture ...and it's big — really, really, really big.

~jeff and jami~

**October 12, 2001**

The MRI was Wednesday. The tumor is basically the same size, maybe a tad bigger the radiologist said. That was good news to us. His symptoms are basically the same. He is just so heavy (he is 60 lbs. now). He is in a wheelchair now because he can only walk a few steps (very wobbly steps) before he is exhausted.

We have had a few "setbacks in hope" in the last few weeks. The neurosurgeon told me that we needed to decide if (in an emergency situation) we want to have a shunt put in or not. In

# Levi's Legacy

other words: Do we want to just cut to the chase and let the inevitable (death) happen sooner since a shunt will only buy time. When he said that I was shocked. I couldn't believe we were at this point of decision making. My feelings toward God were "Okay Lord, you can step in at any time now." Sometimes I feel like I am crying tears of blood because they come from so deep within my soul. It's funny, I used to complain to Jeff about how crazy my life was. I would say, "we need a million dollar life insurance policy for me because if anything ever happened to me you'd have to hire about 50 people to do all I do around here." Now the list of things "to do" is a mere shadow of the new one. But I have discovered that there is something far worse than too much to do… not enough to do. I sometimes say to Jeff, "You know I think I would be a really great mom if it weren't for all these kids and their needs." Ha ha ha ha. But that's not funny anymore.

In this last 2 or 3 weeks the Lord and I have had long conversations. Some good and some bad. But He has heard me and comforted me. His grace has come to me in waves. I'll have 2 or 3 days when I feel as if my heart will burst from the pain. During those days I blindly pursue Him and His word because I need His promises to get through the day. Then, the next 2 or 3 days I feel the burden lifted from me. At that point I have a new understanding of Matthew 11:28-30 *"Come to me, all you who are weary and burdened, and I will give you rest. Take my yoke upon you and learn from me, for I am gentle and humble in heart and you will find rest for your souls. For my yoke is easy and my burden is light."* Sometimes I turn to Him and learn from Him because He is definitely teaching. Other times I turn my head like a rebellious child as if to say, "I don't like you and what you're teaching, your ways are too hard. How could You let me see this happen to my baby? How could You?…I bury my face in the carpet and cry. I don't want His comfort, I want to wallow in my anger and sorrow… but His words come to me and comfort me anyway… *"Though the mountains be shaken and the hills be removed, yet my unfailing love for you will not be shaken nor my covenant of peace be removed. Says the Lord who has compassion for you."* (Isaiah 54:10). Our mountains are being shaken. And we will choose His unfailing love, His covenant of peace. *"He knows the way that I take; when he has tested me, I will come forth as gold. My feet have closely followed His steps; I have kept to his way without turning aside. I have not departed from the commands of his lips; I have treasured the words of his mouth more than my daily bread"* (Job 23:10-12). Lord, let this be true of me. Forgive my childish ways. Give me the strength to grit my teeth and clench my fist in the face of adversity. To stand firm in You… *"Because the Sovereign Lord helps me, I will not be disgraced, Therefore have I set my face like flint, and I know I will not be put to shame. He who vindicates me is near."* (Isaiah 50:7). Lord, let my love and faithfulness to you be in all circumstances, not just the blessings. Let me always *"…look to You, the rock from which I was cut"* (Isaiah 51:1)

A SWEET THING: Caleb's football coaches gave Levi a jersey (#17). Then, they had their team huddle around him. One of the dad/coaches prayed a powerful prayer for him. Then, all the boys lined up and Levi rolled in his wheelchair and gave them "high fives". Then, Monday at practice Frank and Steve (the coaches) brought #17 stickers to put on the back of each of the guys helmets. What a precious way to honor Levi. We are so grateful to the Lord for

32

giving Caleb such special coaches.

~jeff and jami~

## October 18, 2001

On Monday the 15th we had a rough day. The whole night Levi was frustrated. When I would stand him up to go to the bathroom he couldn't stand. He has been having trouble for a while. But it was different; it was much, much worse. He would put his left leg down and fall, immediately. It was completely useless. When we got up in the morning he was really slurring his words badly. I couldn't understand anything he was saying. Somewhere around 10:30 am he started saying he had a headache. Usually when he has headaches they only last a few minutes and then they're gone. But this time it lasted more than an hour and he was wrenched in pain, he wouldn't even touch his head. I made a few calls and started packing us a bag just in case we had to stay the night. I must admit at this point I was wondering if we'd ever leave the hospital. He had gotten so much worse overnight. I was afraid of what the day would hold for us. Jeff came home and we went to the emergency room.

We had a CT scan which showed nothing had changed. Then we had blood work done to see if maybe his electrolytes were off balance and causing this. But the results came back normal. This was good, but a mystery as to why his symptoms were worsening so rapidly. The next day we talked to the doctors at the clinic in Houston and found some answers. According to them the tumor was breaking down. When it breaks down it causes swelling which causes pressure. We had to up the decadron (steroids) a little to keep the swelling down so that he could tolerate a higher dose of the treatment. They told us before this that he would get worse before he got better. But at this rate I wonder if he'll ever get to the "better" part. He is very frustrated and even angry right now. He has to say things 3, 4 even 5 times before we can understand what he's trying to say. He often asks when he's "gonna get better" He is getting so tired of it all. It's so hard to watch him be so frustrated and not be able to help him.

We are so incredibly weary of the constancy of it. With every day there seems to be a new battle. Yesterday we couldn't get any blood out of his broviac. I tried for an hour or more. But nothing. Then, I had a nurse come over and "poke" him but he's so swollen from the steroids she couldn't get a vein; she tried his arms and feet – but nothing. Today, I have to make mega phone calls to find out what my next move is. I'm drowning in my "to do" list. I am so overwhelmed today. Oh Lord, How much longer? We're so tired. We did get a catheter for Levi so that we wouldn't be getting up every hour in the night. But last night it leaked and we were up all night anyway.

So, now you know why this is such a depressing update, I'm running on empty in the sleep area. Yesterday the verse I was clinging to was: Isaiah:64:4; *"Since ancient times no one has heard, no ear has perceived, no eye has seen any God besides you, who acts on behalf of those who wait for Him."* I really love that description of Him. We are trusting that even in the small everyday battles that we face He is refining us and strengthening us. The verse I will claim today is: Ps 94:18&19, (this is good) *"When I said, 'My foot is slipping, ' your love, O Lord, supported me. When anxiety was great within me, your consolation brought joy to my soul."* Please pray for our whole family, we're really at a "low point" today. Thank you. We love you.

~jeff and jami~

## October 22, 2001

I know it hasn't been that long since the last update but I feel like the last one was such a downer I had to tell you something good. On Thursday I talked to the doctor to find out what I should do about the broviac not working properly. She called back and left a message saying I needed to take Levi to the emergency room to get it looked at and possibly have a new line put in. The thought of that overwhelmed me so much that I went outside, laid out a blanket in the front yard and laid down with Levi and Graci and just acted like nothing was said. I stayed there for about 4 hours. I kept thinking, "I really need to go to the emergency room." I couldn't imagine putting Levi through another 7 hour day in the emergency room. I prayed: Lord, you say in your word that your mercies are new every morning. But I kinda feel like it's the same ol' thing the last few days. I can hardly hold my head up. Oh Lord, please show me your mercies anew, I need it so bad.

Later that day we talked to a nurse who told us to try a new way to get the blood out. It worked!!! I have never been so excited to see blood!!! The next day was definitely full of His mercies… Levi woke up with more energy than usual, the lab work went smoothly, I got flowers from my friend (Leslie Johnson) the card read, "To cheer you, even a warrior needs a lift" It was as if it was from the Lord Himself. I also got an e-mail from a lady whose mother was getting treatment in Houston with us. She had gone through a really bad time when they didn't think she was going to make it. But now she is continuously getting better and stronger. Then I got a card from my sister-in-law, Betsy. On the card she wrote this verse: *"The Lord longs to be gracious to you and waits on high to have compassion on you… blessed are all those who long for Him."* Isaiah 30:18 The whole day was filled with little "acts of love" from my Heavenly Father. So blatantly from Him. I could never deny that He is active and working in my life. His mercies are new every morning. It's as if He lets me feel the pressures of my circumstances so tightly only to push me to cry out to Him for help so that He can shower us with His blessings. He has shown Himself to be personal and active and so faithful. Who could deny His goodness? Who could deny that He is a God that acts on behalf of His people?

*"…and for this reason I kneel before the Father and pray that you, through our lives, would be able to grasp how wide and long and high and deep is the love of Christ, and to know this love that surpasses knowledge – that you may be filled to the measure of all the fullness of God… To Him who is able to do immeasurably more than all we ask or imagine… to Him be glory in Christ Jesus throughout all generations, for ever and*

# Levi's Legacy

*ever!"* Ephesians 3:17-21

Thank you all so much for going to the throne of grace on our behalf. We felt it like you would not believe. Blessings to you.

~jeff and jami~

## October 29, 2001

The other day I was driving through a wealthy neighborhood, I noticed how many gazebos, benches, hammocks, swings, big beautiful trees to sit under there were, things I call "memory makers". But nobody was out there. There were no children sitting on benches with their dads. There were no mommies reading to little ones under trees and on hammocks. Such possibilities. So many life changing talks waiting to be had. So many missed opportunities. I know why. All the mommies and daddies are waiting for the perfect moment to go out to the bench, hammock, swing to just "be" with their children. But the demands of life are too strong and perfect moments are too hard to find. I am learning from empty gazebos. When I see a place that could be a memory, a moment of life changing proportion I am going to stop and get in it, sit on it, swing on it, sit under it and just "be". You know why? Because I can.

About a week ago Levi and I were driving along the road. He started crying from the back seat. I said, "Levi, what's wrong?" He said in a whimper, "I just need to hug you" (sweet, precious little man of mine). I pulled over in a neighborhood and parked on the side of the street and got out of the car, opened his door and we hugged. Cars drove by and people stared, they slowed down and tried to figure out what I was doing. But we were busy. We were making a memory. It was beautiful. I almost missed it because we were so close to home. I almost said "can you just wait until we get home?" But that would have been a big mistake because those kind of moments don't wait. You have to grab them while you can. Now, every time we drive by that neighborhood he yells out "hey, that's where we hugged, that's where you stopped and hugged me!"

Just 7 months ago Levi was perfectly healthy as far as we knew and if he had cried and said "I just want to hug you" I probably would have been more "practical" and said, just wait a few more streets until we get home and then I'll hug you. But not now—I know that we might not make it to the next street so we stop right away. Not just for Levi but Caleb, Jonah and Graci too. Isn't that who Jesus was? Didn't he stop at any given moment to "be" with people? His disciples probably thought it would have been more practical to wait until the time was more "appropriate." But not my Jesus, no, right away was good for Him. He didn't want to miss the moment. And neither do I.

A PAINFUL CONVERSATION SHOWS THAT I MISSED A FEW MOMENTS ALONG THE WAY:

Caleb – "I wish Levi didn't have a brain tumor."

Me – "Me too, what are your reasons for saying that?" (I was just wanting to see his heart,

35

not knowing what I would see.)

Caleb – "Well, I'm tired of seeing Levi hurting and I don't want him to have cancer anymore. And so you would love me more again."

Me – Painful silence.

We talked more about it later and I reassured him that my love for him had not changed. But you know what? All he knew is that most of my attention goes to caring for Levi and he felt left out. You know what's worse that someone being "dis"enchanted with you? Someone that is "un"enchanted with you. And I think that's what he felt. I was just too busy to show them that they are so "cool" to me. We have made some changes around here, good ones. Our house is a little messier (okay, alot) and we're late alot. But we're feeling alot more love

### November 5 , 2001

Today Levi is doing fairly well. Yesterday he was very lethargic. Last night we were playing a board game and he just stared at me the whole time, as if he were looking right through me. We stopped the game and prayed over him. Jonah prayed first, "Lord, would you heal Levi and make him better soon? will you make his tumor go away?" Caleb prayed, "Lord, would you make Levi 'regular' again? Help him to be able to run and play baseball again? Make him better, please. amen." Wow, I couldn't have said it better myself. The last couple of days have been hard for us. We've just been sad. I mean what else can you be but sad when you watch your four year old boy struggle to eat, go to the bathroom, play a game. Everything is difficult for him. Yesterday Graci had a new pink dress on with white tights and black patent leather shoes. She looked down at herself and said, "Mommy, I look beautiful today, I want to dance." Then she turned and looked at Levi and said, "Levi, I want to dance with you." Usually, Levi would have been so excited about the offer. But this time he looked at her with an irritated smirk and said "I can't dance, I can't walk." But then she couldn't understand him so she had to say "what?" about 3 times. Needless to say he was in tears by the end of that conversation.

He is so heavy and swollen. I feel like I'm missing out on him growing up because he's growing up in a bubble and I can't see him. If he ever does recover and lose all this weight I will still have missed out on so much of his growing up. And then I reprimand myself and say, "Quit being so greedy... you should be grateful for any time you get with him." Some days I miss his old face and his old body. I look at pictures and mourn. But then other times I think of how much I will miss his chubby little face. When I pick him up (which is getting harder and harder at 63 lbs. now) and he is so smushy and soft I think I will miss that too. Then I think, "Oh Lord If you take him I will miss 'both' of him, the old 'little' Levi and the new 'chubby' Levi. I can't bare the thought of it. I am split in two. I can't stand to see him live this way and pray that you {Jesus} would take him soon so that he would be free from this misery". But then quickly I take it back and selfishly say "NO!" "I can't live without him". It is hard, this new life, but I'll take it over the option of not having him here. How did I get to this place of bartering, in my mind, for the life of my son? As if God makes deals. I know my heavenly Father is love and His heart breaks as He watches us fumble around in the dark learning to trust, learning not to depend on what we see in the light but what we know to be true in our hearts regardless of the cruel darkness. I know He longs to show the whole picture to us but He must wait. He is doing something. He has a plan and we must trust that it is good. In some ways trusting is harder than ever because so much is at stake. But in other ways it is easier to trust because He has never been anything but faithful. We are learning that this is not a sprint but a marathon. A friend (John Shultis) gave us a book called "A Long Obedience In The Same Direction." The title speaks for itself. We are learning that it's the long battles, the hardest things in life that make life worth living. It is not for the "strong" it's for the weak at heart like us that can do nothing but fall into the strength of the Father. Beth Moore says, "We cannot choose whether or not we will have fire in our lives but we can choose whether or not we will be refined by it."

~jeff and jami~


**November 16, 2001**

It's been 5 "sweet Novembers" since the Lord first lent us our little man. The day of his birthday was not that great though. He wasn't feeling very well, and was having one of those "seizure days." (About a week ago he was incoherent, his responses were delayed by about 3 seconds and he would look right through you, we found out later that those are little seizures that sometimes last 2 hours.) About two weeks before his birthday he made a comment to me that makes me believe his "big day" was a disappointment to him: I said, "Are you excited about your big #5 birthday?" He said, "Yeah, because I won't have this (pointing to his broviac tubes)." I had to be the bearer of bad news and tell him that the tubes would have to stay. His bottom lip poked out and his shoulders fell in huge disappointment. For some reason he thought that since it was his birthday we would take out the broviac and he would be "done" with it, he would be "regular" (in Caleb's words) again. Oh how I wished and dreamed. But the battle goes on, it is no respecter of "special days."

Levi loves to watch himself on home videos, so we watched some. I was not prepared for the rush of emotion that came with it. Watching him play and be silly in his "other" body. It was so weird, I missed him and his old body more than ever. He looked in excitement at the TV and said, "Hey, that's when my arm was 'on'". That day/moment sparked a wrestling match between God and me. It's been about 3 days of total torment. The pain, anguish, sorrow and weariness that is in my heart could never find appropriate expression. For 2 days I wouldn't talk to HIM. I was angry that He would not take this from us. Why? How much longer? I am so weary of the "on and on-ness" of it. I have believed that I was created to be God's "friend", to enjoy Him, to find satisfaction in Him and His ways... but the last three days I have given Him the cold shoulder (I did NOT turn my back on Him but I toiled, argued and gritted my teeth at Him). I wanted to fight, kick, punch, yell, scream and spit. I had a "Jacob moment." I am still so weak and tattered from the match. But our relationship (the Lord and I) is on it's way to a new depth that can only come from "dukin' it out", from honesty and transparency, however brutal it may be …my "hallelujah's" are weak and muted today. I am broken, turned inside out, desperate, I can't understand all that He allows, I just can't see the reason, but my life is in His hands and though I can't see Him I choose to trust Him. Even though my heart is torn I will praise Him. Even though I feel deserted, I will praise Him. Even in the darkest valley. My world is shattered and it seems all hope is gone. We will trust You in our loneliness. How could we be worthy to carry His name if we didn't trust Him in times of great darkness? Is this a preparation for the days ahead when our faith will be tested far beyond what we can imagine now? We will not forget that You hung on a cross, that You bled and died for us… that if we join You in Your suffering we will also join You in the blessings…

When there's something on TV that I think would be too hard for my children to see I quickly cover their eyes so that their minds and hearts would not have to bear something that would harden them. I sometimes wish the Lord would put His hand over my eyes… I don't want to see it. This is hard to watch, my son's body swelling, his face paralyzed on the left side, unable to walk, run, play, see. Everywhere we go people stare at him (and he definitely notices)… oh Lord, turn it off. It's a bad show and my heart and mind are too fragile and young to bear it… but it goes on and on… He leaves it on… why? I don't know. But I still choose Him in this. Oh that He would reign in us in our darkest hour.

In my psychological and spiritual breakdown, the wrestling match to beat all… Jeff has proven to be my "knight in shining armor." When I would call him (and I did, way more than just a few times) and say "I can't do it today, it's too much…I'm falling apart…" He would drop everything and come home to help me, listen to me yell at God, watch me throw things, kick things and hold me while I sobbed uncontrollably. He had no idea what he was getting into on that day he said "I do." He has truly seen the best and worst and still, miraculously chooses to stay [smile]. The Lord knew I needed such a man for such a time as this and I praise Him for that.

I hope this update and the reality of the battle didn't scare you away. Truth really stinks sometimes, doesn't it? The truth is… life is hard, sometimes unbearable; people get sick, people die, evil is rampant, there is a devil and he hates you and me… but the other side of truth is that there is a God who can handle it all…

~jami~


## November 18, 2001

1:50 PM – Yesterday Levi went into what appeared to be a coma. Jami called 911; the paramedics and fire truck were there in minutes and transported him to the nearest hospital, where they decided to "Life-Flight" him to Emory. There he got a CAT scan, which indicated no change since the previous one (good news). They say he did not slip into a coma, but are theorizing other causes for the loss of normal body functions. Presently (1:50 PM) Levi is in intensive care and considered critical, he has fluid in his lungs and needs help in breathing.

Please petition God to raise him up by His mighty resurrection power, and receive glory beyond anything we've ever seen! And pray for strength for Jami and Jeff.

10:00 PM – The previous (hastily written) report needs a few corrections and additions, namely 1) it was Egleston Children's Hospital, not Emory; 2) his condition this morning included a very low oxygen level requiring heavy respiration, 3) in addition to the fluid in his lungs, he was unable to eliminate.

After church today, two of our precious prayer warriors, Jacquie Tyre and Barbara Johnson, headed for the hospital armed with the Word and faith in the God of the impossible. They asked Jeff to read from 1 Kings 17:17-24, then prayed over him with this passage as a model and anointed him with Frankincense oil while Jacquie sang to the Lord. Shortly after this, the nurses came back into the room to find Levi's oxygen level had started to improve, he had had a major bowel movement (a real stinker according to Jeff!) and the fluid in his lungs was all gone! This really surprised the nurses! What a turning point it was! Jeff and Jami are convinced this was ordained of the Lord, and are much encouraged and refreshed by His obvious answer to prayer. Take a moment to review the prayer strategies Jacquie has offered , based on this experience. Thank you Barbara and Jacquie! …and thank all of you who have been faithfully lifting up Levi all these months.

Mel

## November 19, 2001

As the two updates of November 18th indicated, Levi was admitted to Egleston Children's Hospital on Saturday in critical condition. He has been in ICU since then. Yesterday (Monday) afternoon the doctors made it clear that they believed Levi had less than a week to live. Needless to say that brought a heaviness to Jeff and Jami and the rest of us around them.

But after letting it sink in for awhile as we all silently kept watch over him, while trying to console one another, the secret feelings – first of Jami, then of Jeff and finally, one by one, of other family members and friends – began to pour out as prayers of desperation. For the next hour or so (we lost track of time), as we all drew closer to the heart of God, the Holy Spirit seemed to be coaching us how to pray: more and more our desperate cries began to blossom into expressions of confident trust in our faithful, loving God. It was powerful – the Lord seemed to be pleased with our earnest petitions to preserve Levi's life from the vicious attacks of the Destroyer.

Afterward, his blood pressure – the second, lower number (diastolic) – which had dropped down into the danger zone only minutes before, was now normal! He moved his leg, then his arm, then in response to questions, nodded his head and partially opened his eyes, which for months had been badly crossed but now were looking normal! These were all very encouraging signs. We believe – now more than ever – that God wants to use Levi in some important way, and that the enemy does not want that to happen.

I think one of the lessons we need to take out of this is, since *"…the effectual fervent prayer of a righteous man availeth much"* (James 5:16), God is patiently waiting for us to participate in accomplishing the wonderful things He already wants to do in our midst, so the world will see and give Him the glory and humbly bow before Him and, placing their trust in Jesus, receive the Gift of God – eternal life. But He insists on waiting for us to join Him in this Master Plan by first praying – fervently; not to twist His arm to do something He's reluctant to do, but to get us involved in the process for our ultimate good. What an amazing God!!

Thank you for participating in this way on behalf of my grandson, Levi and his mother and father. Please, don't let up!

Mel


## November 20, 2001

Please join us in fervent prayer!

As I come before the Lord with a tormented soul today...I claim these verses and ask that you would come along with us in prayer for the "little man" today. 1 Kings 17:17-24, Luke 18:1-8, Oh Lord, would you not bring about justice for your chosen ones? Will You not honor our persistent quest for healing? We come before you day and night with pain, anguish and wailing in our souls. Guide us in your truth, show us your ways. Draw near to us because we are drawing near to You... we humble ourselves in Your sight... we will lift up Your name...

"THE FATHER USES HUNGER BORN OUT OF DESPERATION TO WEAN US FROM THE WORLD AND MAKE US ADDICTED TO HIM"

It is true—we see this world has nothing for us. It is useless to us. Come along with us and see that the Lord is good... Please come to the throne of mercy and grace on our behalf, please be persistent in your cries to Him that He would allow us to have our "little man" a little longer. With a holy tenacity we say along with Jacob, "We will not let go of Him until He blesses us." ...In the end may we "come forth as gold" (Job 23:9-12).

~jeff and jami~


## November 22, 2001 – Thanksgiving Day

Wow. This is a day like no other...I am in my favorite place... the secret place that my Father calls me to. I need this place like never before. I come here to beg for the strength to continue in this battle for the life of my precious little man. When I stay at the hospital too long without coming out to be alone, completely alone with the Lord I become angry (very, very angry). Yesterday the nurses came in to suction his lungs out. They stick a tube down his ventilator and kinda "vacuum" out his lungs. His face showed anguish and tears were rolling down his face into his ears. I was so angry at God. How much more must he endure? The doctors were trying to get a response from his brain so they shot ice water into his ears... nothing. He didn't even flinch. Oh God have mercy... anger blew through me. Jeff and I prayed that the Lord would give me some kind of vision, some kind of something to help me go on in this. I am at the point of giving up, letting go. But I can't. I must hope. I must. How could I give up. His own mother giving up...shame on me...This morning when I woke up the Lord was generous and gave me a picture in my fragile mind. A vision of a lion mauling a child (I assume it was a representation of my little man). If a literal lion were attacking my "man" would I give up and just say "Oh well, he's a gonner..." or would I run after the lion kicking, punching, searching for some sort of a weapon for that particular battle? YES!! I would not walk away. I would continue to fight. This is a battle like no other. The Lord has an incredible plan for Levi's life and the "Lion" is afraid of it. It must be a really big plan. He is not easily loosening his grip. I know the world or even those believers of little faith will mock us or even think we're "overboard" on this "hope thing".

Please join us in fighting in the spiritual realm. Please don't give up. Please, press on with us. The doctors say 2 days to a week is all he has left but claim with us that our God does not submit to the limitations of time and medical predictions. Our God is a passionate and merciful God, longing to "romance" us by healing Levi. We will take today and not look to tomorrow. We are eternally grateful for the 5 "sweet Novembers" we've been given but we confess we are greedy and will ask for more and more. We pray that Levi will soon say. "I WILL NOT DIE BUT LIVE. AND WILL PROCLAIM WHAT THE LORD HAS DONE." Psalm 118:17.

More desperate than ever for the"saints" of God to boldly join us...

~jeff and jami~

**November 23, 2001**

New Urgent Prayer Request

Levi has been on a respirator for the past week. This evening they removed the respirator which was a traumatic and life-threatening event. He is now on a ventilator which is intended to enable him to make the transition to breathing on his own – but he's not there yet. Please pray that God would give him the ability to breathe on his own very soon so that he will not have to be re-intubated (respirator reinserted). This would, in effect, be acknowledging defeat, because it would mean he could only breathe normally with the help of a machine.

Also, please remember Levi's parents, Jeff & Jami and the extended family, that God would wrap His arms of love around each one and give them rest, wisdom, strength and peace.

Grandaddy's personal note –

I see this as a spiritual battle. Levi is the battlefield. The enemy clearly wants to destroy him because he knows something about Levi's future ministry that we don't know, and he has had some success over the past eight months, and particularly over this last week as Levi has been on life-support (the doctors are giving him only days at best). But I believe God wants to use him – more than He already has. I could be wrong but I have this strong recurring mental picture of the enemy attacking him and the "good guys" (angels) defending him – but only while there is sufficient prayer support. I'm thinking of Exodus 17:11-12: *"And it came to pass, when Moses held up his hand, that Israel prevailed: and when he let down his hand, Amalek prevailed. But Moses' hands were heavy; and they took a stone, and put it under him, and he sat thereon; and Aaron and Hur stayed up his hands, the one on the one side, and the other on the other side; and his hands were steady until the going down of the sun".*

I really think the Lord wants to train us all to be better prayer warriors, *"...For we wrestle not against flesh and blood, but against principalities, against powers, against the rulers of the darkness of this world, against spiritual wickedness in high places."* – Eph. 6:12.

If this picture represents what's really going on in the unseen world, then would you join us in asking the Father to strengthen the hands of the front-line troops, those mighty angels of God, that they may completely vanquish the enemy and rescue Levi from certain death, that God would restore him to perfect health, and that he would be protected from further physical problems so he could grow up to become the man of God he is destined to be. This vision keeps me motivated. Maybe it will help you too.

Thank you so, so much for loving and praying for Levi. I am convinced God is doing more than we know through his young life as he and his family continue this struggle.

Mel

### November 24, 2001

I just spoke with Jeff at the hospital, where they had just finished a meeting with the doctors and decided not to reintubate him when they remove the ventilator, even though they know (humanly speaking) Levi will most likely not be able to breathe on his own – the only "life-support system" they are interested in is the non-artificial one that God provides!

Right now they are making plans to get set up with hospice service, bring him home and have the elders anoint him with oil and pray over him; they are acting in obedient faith on the basis of the clear instruction and promise in God's own Holy Word (in James 5:14, 15). They are believing the promise that "the prayer of faith shall save the sick" and expecting the Lord to raise him up, as He said He would.

In Hi s hands,

Mel

### November 26, 2001

It's Monday. We brought Levi home from the hospital via a transport ambulance yesterday. Finally!! He's home. The time at the hospital was extremely difficult. Hope was hard to keep. We would come before the Lord and ask for an extra measure of faith, we would feel His presence and strength but then we would have to have (another) meeting with the doctors.

What a hard job they have. We would go over the facts and the facts are that naturally speaking Levi will not live. He will continue to deteriorate until he dies and that according to medicine will be soon, very soon (days). We would leave those "meetings" completely defeated. In my mind I would see him struggle for his last breath, I would try not to let my mind go there but the darkness was too strong. ...~jami~

We wept by his bedside very regularly all week long (8 days in ICU). The hard part was/is looking at the pictures of our kids together (cohesive), I cry now thinking about the perfect memories we have of our Levi. He now lays still, little response, in a hospital bed in our bedroom.

We chose to leave ICU early and to have home hospice care so that Levi could be at home in our home environment. For the sake of time now I must leave many details out about the friends we made with many of the staff there at Egleston ICU, but thank you for caring and pouring your hearts into Levi while he was there.

We came home Sunday at 1:30 with the urgent purpose of calling the elders of the church and anointing Levi with oil and praying over him in faith. James 5:14-15. We believe that God will raise him up.

From the time we started praying at 2:15 until now there has not stopped being intercessors in our house, even early hours of the night and morning. There is an urgency to see Levi healed and raised up. Even now there is intercessory prayer going on with pastors all over Atlanta here in our house CRYING OUT TO GOD. There is no time for grieving now, we are fighting for his life against the devil in agreement with GOD'S WORD THE BIBLE. We are claiming Psalms 118:17 for Levi's life – *"I shall not die, but live, and declare the works of God"*.

Please fight with us and go to the Father for Levi's healing. Even come and pray if the Holy Spirit leads.

There is absolutely nothing that any man can do now to save Levi's life...and maybe that's why it has come all the way to this point 8 months later...so that God gets 100% of the glory.

We will update real soon.

Jeff

### November 28, 2001

I know there are so many of you who are feeling "in the dark" and want to know what in the world happened. I'll give you a quick overview: On the Saturday before Thanksgiving we had a wonderful morning. We all just stayed home together. There was no place we had to be and that is a rare thing for us. Levi wasn't feeling that great and wasn't hungry at all which was really different. In the early afternoon he threw up. We knew this was really bad and meant that the ventricles (which bring fluid from the spine to the brain) were swollen and blocking the flow. He was still coherent though so I was hoping maybe it was just a virus. I put on some shorts and a T-shirt and got in the tub with him and held him in my lap because he was "wobbly". Jeff went to get him a drink and Caleb and I were just talking to him. All of a sudden he said "Uh oh, Uh oh, I feel funny" and immediately stopped breathing. Caleb ran to get Jeff. We carried his sweet little limp body to the bed and were trying to get some sort of response out of him. He started to breathe off and on but very sporadically. He began to throw up again, and again. We were terrified. As I was on the bed holding him Jeff laid down (prostrate) on the floor and began to cry out to God. "Please Lord, have mercy on our son, Please God don't take him..." We called the ambulance and they were there in probably 3 minutes. They rushed him to Gwinnett Medical Center because it was the closest. Then they Life-Flighted him from there to Egelston Children's Hospital. We were so afraid. After this long eight month battle was it all over now? I was so weary from the constancy of the practical side of the "fight" but I would do it all over again and again if I was given the choice. My heart groaned to my heavenly Father prayers that I couldn't pray on my own. But in the midst of this long nightmare it was the deepest desire of our heart, soul and spirit to praise the Lord through it all. Even now when hope was so far away, He, in His kindness, brought me to a place of praise to Him. "Help us Lord, to praise you, no matter what happens today..."

Levi was in intensive care. In the next eight days we would "go places we did not want to go"...We had countless "meetings" with the doctors – sometimes 3 or 4 a day (I loved all the doctors but I hated the meetings because there was no good news). At one time we were told that Levi was doing so badly that they couldn't say that he would live the next 5 minutes. We had to make big (really big) decisions. We had to decide if we would resuscitate and gain a few more days maybe weeks or just release him into the hand of the Lord. We chose the latter. After much prayer we knew that we must completely "let go" and see the Lord do His work. But, we went boldly before His throne (as He has called us to do) and claimed His word for Levi's complete healing. We are not in denial. We are simply believing that our God is THE great physician and is more than able to bring complete renewal to Levi's body...

After meeting with the doctors on Saturday we decided to transport Levi home with no order to resuscitate. There was no reason to believe (naturally speaking) that Levi would live through the night. We told the hospital staff that it was our desire to get him to our house so he could die at home (and in no pain). It was a risk to transport... but in our hearts before the Lord of Life, our intention was to get him home to LIVE... to surround Him with the body of Christ, the elders, friends and family that believe that our God heals. As soon as we got home and in the house he turned blue and stopped breathing... But as this was happening people were coming in to pray. The elders came and anointed him with oil (in obedience to scripture) The Holy Spirit came... Levi started to breathe again. It has been touch and go but our house has been a revolving door of prayer. People come and go day and night lifting our little man up in powerful, believing prayer...

BUT THERE'S A GREATER MESSAGE THAT THE LORD HAS BROUGHT IN OUR SEEKING ...AND IT'S FOR YOU, THE BODY OF CHRIST, THE TRUE CHURCH OF CHRIST OUR KING ...SO LISTEN UP!!!!!!!!!!!!!! IT'S GOOD STUFF.

# Levi's Legacy

There is a picture here that the Lord has given. Levi's body has a tumor, a cancer that is growing in him; it has, over the past eight months gained strength, taking over and weakening his sweet body. There is also a tumor/cancer that grows in the body of Christ. It too has gained strength and power. How? Because we have forgotten our first love. We have become "familiar" with His holiness. We have begun to think that we understand Him, that we know all there is to know of Him. We are prideful before an All Powerful, All knowing God and we are not afraid. "Woe to us"... The tumor in the "body" is complacency and boredom. We have not pursued Him. We only want the benefits but not the sacrifice. It is time to come humbly before God Almighty and repent, yeah that's right – repent. If we have an "attitude" toward that word we might want to "get over it" because that's where it's at. He is kind and gentle, wanting to bless us, He is above all things, above all the ways of men, above all kingdoms, above all wonders the world has ever known, all wealth and treasures of the earth. And He calls us to recognize our sinfulness before Him (repent) for one reason... So, He can embrace us and show us more of His goodness. Oh that we would be forever desperate for You, Lord. That you would be the air we breathe, that we would recognize that we are lost without You. That our satisfaction would be found in walking in Your Holy Presence. Oh Lord, help us, forgive us, heal us. Open the floodgates of Heaven and let it rain your healing. Righteousness and Justice are the foundation of Your throne, Oh Lord. Some day soon every knee will bow and every tongue confess that You, Jesus Christ are Lord! ...Ahhhhh I love the thought of that.

In the last eight months we have seen God anew. It has been painful and even horrible. We have felt at times that we could not withstand a minute more ...But we consider it all worth it if our Lord and Saviour Jesus has been exalted, if you have seen even a glimpse of Him through our frail humanness, if you have taken even one step closer to pursuing the "beautiful mystery" that is Him. We stand in our fatigue and weakness and shout that our God is an Awesome God, He reigns in Heaven above, all wisdom and power and glory are His. He is the worthy Lamb... No matter what the days ahead may hold... We will continue our quest for intimacy with the Father. We refuse to be denied the "Highest things of God."

Levi is opening his eyes, he is responding to questions by nodding his head (he cannot talk) he is moving his right arm and leg occasionally and breathing on his own with much help from an oxygen mask. There is not much more to tell. But we will keep you posted as the days go by. Please know that we are eternally grateful for each one of you and all you have done. Even if you just check the website every once in a while because you care. We are blessed just to know that you are interested. Please press on in prayer ...the battle rages on... we love you.

*"Now to Him who is able to keep you from stumbling. And to present you faultless before the presence of His glory with exceeding joy..."* (Jude 1:24)

~jeff and jami~

P.S. Please pray for Caleb, Jonah and Graci (and me) I miss them so terribly and want so badly to be with them, hold them, love them and cry with them but I can't right now and it's killing me.

## December 1, 2001

It's Saturday morning. A week ago today we were in the hospital wondering what the next minutes/hours would hold for us and our little man. A lifetime has occurred since then... Today he is watching a video ("The Miracles of Jesus", which is very appropriate) with his Uncle Dicky. The doctors* cannot explain why he is still alive, but we can: our God still acts on behalf of His people. There is still much prayer needed so please don't stop. But can I tell you what I have learned in the last week about prayer? It thrills the Father when we come before Him just seeking His face, to know Him anew, to "behold His beauty". When we come boldly yet humbly before Him asking Him to captivate our hearts and teach us something new about His character. When we say "Oh Father, maximize my pleasure in You, I am a glutton for your presence... Oh how my heart and soul sing knowing that people all over are coming into the Holy of Holies to meet with God, drink from His never-ending fountain, being forever changed into the likeness of Him while they are praying for Levi. That's the biggest miracle of all. What an incredible honor to be used by the Lord to open many eyes to see Him in a different light. We are in constant awe... We delight in the works of His hands because our "god box" is being blown away...

On Tuesday morning at about 1:00am Jeff, Lori and I were praying over Levi, claiming scripture on his behalf... I read Psalm 70 out loud... *"Hasten, O God, to save me; O Lord, come quickly to help me... You are my help and my deliverer; O Lord, do not delay."* Immediately after I finished reading Levi opened his eyes and put his arm up for a hug. It was incredible to say the least. On Friday morning about 1:00am he pulled out his NG tube (feeding tube) and said, "I'm hungry." His first request was for chips and salsa. We decided it might be better if we start with something a little less "pokey" on his throat. He's been drinking a lot of juice and water and eating soft foods. It is still hard to understand him when he talks and his throat is very sore from the ventilator. He can't use his left side and is unable to sit up YET. Please continue to pray with us for his complete recovery. Isn't it incredible????? He was basically dead on Sunday and today HE LIVES. How 'bout God? Just when we thought we had Him all figured out He goes and gets wild and crazy on us!!!!!! GO GOD!!!!!!!!!

*"My soul will boast in the Lord; let the afflicted hear and rejoice. Glorify the Lord with me; let us exalt His name together..."* Psalm 34:2-3

* Our doctors are believers. They believe that this is a miracle. They give God all the glory... Dr. Fitzgerald-Soapes (Aunt Jan to my kids) spent the night at our house for the first 4 nights we were home and stayed up all through the night with Levi so that Jeff and I could rest. After being such close friends/family for so many years how could we have known how incredible she really is? We are still amazed... Dr. Fortenberry was the ICU doctor the night before we left the hospital. He is the doctor that had to meet with us and plan the dreaded transport home. He prayed and cried with us the very first day we met him. He came home with us on the transport. He came back the next day and stayed with us for 10 hours. He has been back to see Levi almost everyday since. He has turned out to be one of the finest men we have known. A blessing.

~jeff and jami~

# Levi's Legacy

## December 6, 2001

Today finds me really discouraged. I know, I know – I should be soooo grateful for the healing that we have seen. I guess I have become greedy. I am an American Christian and have been tainted by the fast-food, "hurry up" lifestyle. I am so ready for Levi's complete recovery. His mind is as sharp as a tack and he is so ready to have the abilities of his lower body restored fully. He wants to go out to breakfast. He wants to go upstairs to his room, he wants to go outside and play …he keeps forgetting that his body doesn't work yet. It's a strange thing to be half way through a healing. You can't call the doctors and say "hey, his legs still don't work", because technically he should be dead. Weird, huh? The only one I can talk to about this "purgatory" I feel like we're in is God Himself. So, (of course) I do… David's Psalms are the cry of my heart, *"Answer me when I call to you, Oh my righteous God. Give me relief from my distress; be merciful to me and hear my prayer."* (Psalm 4:1) *"Give ear to my words, O Lord, consider my sighing. Listen to my cry for help, my King and my God for to you I pray."* (Psalm 5:1 & 2)

I went for a run around our neighborhood today… I ran past the pool and a flood of memories came over me. I wasn't prepared for it. All of a sudden I saw (in my minds eye) all the kids playing in the water. Levi in his swimmies and goggles, his swimming trunks falling down. His hair was bleached white from the sun, he was tan and freckled on his sweet little nose …laughing, playing, having fun with the other kids. Oh how I miss that …I remember when I could give equal time to each of my children. Gone are those days. I hardly know my other children now. All my time is devoted to taking care of one. Lord, help Caleb, Jonah and Graci to know how much I love them and miss them. Help them to survive these "never ending" days. I know the Lord is preserving them but my "mothers heart" is breaking to enjoy them, to be able to focus on them. Oh Holy breath of Heaven revive my heart. I am so weary and dry. I am spent …I know that this whole healing/waiting process is divinely orchestrated and that the Father is closer than I realize so I press into Him in my barrenness and brokenness, longing for a deeper awareness of His presence… Just when I think I have "fought the good fight" it goes on and on and on…

In S. J. Hills book Personal Revival, he tells this story: There once was a young man who, in his search for God, came to study at the feet of a wise man. One day the teacher took his pupil to a lake and led him out into shoulder-deep water. Placing his hands on the student's head, he suddenly pushed him under the water and held him there until the young man, in desperation fought his way to the surface. In utter shock and confusion, the student stared at the old man as if to ask, "What in the world are you doing?" The teacher, in response, looked at his pupil and said, "When you want God as much as you wanted air, you shall find Him." That's where we are now!!! We want HIM. Not just Levi's complete restoration …HIS presence to be continuously with us.

Our lives are forever changed, we have seen the Mighty Hand of God bring healing to our house, we felt His presence sweep through us and we cannot – we will not – live without the constant "welcome mat" for His presence. I think that's it!!! He wants us to be desperately seeking a deeper revelation of Him. Never being satisfied with what we had of Him today but looking to tomorrow expectantly to see Him in new light again... What you're seeing here is deep crying out to deep* (Psalm 42:7).

I know this is one crazy mixed up update, breaking all the "literary rules" but I am one crazy mixed up "rule breaker."

~jami~


**December 9, 2001**

It's early Sunday morning and I'm here in "the secret place." The last update was a down hearted one so I just wanted to let you know that the Lord, once again has comforted me. He has shown me "just enough light for the step I'm on" and is in control of the ones ahead. This morning I was reading in my journal [from November 25], the day we transported Levi home. I wanted to see how far the Lord has brought us...

> 10:20am ...with each breath I watch him (Levi) take, I say to the Lord, "just one more, just one more... until I look at the clock and realize that I've been watching him breathe for hours."

> 1:30pm ...they're taking out all the I.V.s now. They know he probably won't make the trip home. (What a sad job.) Oh Lord, help him to be comfortable. Hold him and don't let go... Help me – how will I get out of this hospital without falling to pieces?...

> ...time is cruel and indecent without understanding how desperately I need it to stop. "Just wait one more minute so I can hold him while he's alive."

> ...I know that there have been mothers down through history who have watched their children die. But they couldn't possibly have loved them as much as I love mine. It's just not possible. Surely no one has ever hurt as badly as I do right now...

When I read these I was reminded of how mighty and wonderful and merciful the Lord has been. He has brought us so far. Who is like our God? *"...but I, by your great mercy, will come into your house; in reverence will I bow down toward your holy temple."* (Psalm 5:7). Time and time again He proves Himself to be a God that does not forget or forsake. And time and time again I am a woman of little faith having to be reminded of His Goodness and never ending Faithfulness to us. Rubem Alves says: "Hope is hearing the melody of the future. Faith is to dance to it." I am learning to dance. I'm learning to be boldly confident in the Lord. I'm learning that He is not like me in that He stays on track with His character, He doesn't "get down" and want to give up... and the coolest thing I'm learning is that He delights in me. I don't know why because I'm not very delightful but I'll take it anyway...

*"He reached down from on high and took hold of me; He drew me out of deep waters He rescued me from my powerful enemy, from my foes who were too strong for me... the Lord was my support. He brought me out into the spacious place; He rescued me because he delighted in me." Psalm 18:16-19*

I know there's a lot more to learn, but for today I'm basking in this lesson because it's a fun one!!!!

~jami~

## December 15, 2001

Last time I wrote you I didn't give you any practical information about Levi and his improvement. I'm sorry. I must admit it's hard to write about his daily improvement because it's so gradual. I wish I could write an update telling you about how he's out running and playing in the front yard... but not today, maybe tomorrow!!!!!! He is definitely getting stronger and stronger every day. It's just very hard to notice when I'm with him 24/7. He can sit up with help from pillows. He can take a bath without me holding him up. He is very alert mentally but obviously frustrated when we can't understand what he's trying to tell us. He's trapped inside this shell that is not serving him well. But this too will soon pass. I am slowly bringing him off the decadron. When we came home from the hospital he was on 4mg every 12 hours. Today I started him on 1/2mg every 12 hours. So, hopefully, his appetite will dwindle and he will lose a little weight and be more comfortable. Since he is so sedentary he gets constipated. We pray the "poopie prayer" quite often (isn't that cool that God is a God who hears us when we ask for a healing and when we ask for a "poop?")

Our days are hard and seem to go on forever at times. But in the midst of waiting (for the promise of complete restoration) we have had some cool moments... since Levi has a hard time feeding himself, Caleb, Jonah and Graci like to feed him. Graci was feeding him lunch yesterday. I went down to the basement for a second. When I came back up Levi was covered (I mean COVERED) with tuna. Graci couldn't understand what he was saying... He was saying "you're making me laugh" but she thought he was saying "could you go fast" so she did. He was chewing as fast as he could and she was "shoveling" as fast as she could. You gotta love that!!!!!!!!

Last night we went out to eat because Levi was dying to go to Chili's for some chips and salsa. So, we packed him up and took him and Graci (Caleb and Jonah were spending the night with the Hartley's). It was a really weird moment because from the time we walked in, to the time we left, people were staring at us. If they only knew that just 9 months ago they would have been staring because he was such a beautiful child but now they were staring out of pity... If they only knew that he was saved from death just three weeks ago they would have been staring because they were looking at a miracle, the mercy of God personified.

...Levi just called Jeff and said "Dad, I want to wrestle you and I'm gonna beat you, because I'm strong" ...so gotta go!!!

Here's the verse we're claiming today... *"I will strengthen them in the Lord and in his name they will walk...declares the Lord."* Zechariah 10:12

~jami~

## December 20, 2001 (11:18 AM)

It's December 20th, my twin sister, Lori's 36th birthday (and mine too). So far it has been a rough one. Yesterday Levi had a really bad day: difficulty breathing, not eating all day and just generally frustrated with his situation. We had a group of prayer warriors come last night and it was an incredible time of the Lord meeting us there. Levi was breathing much easier and seemed fine. We went to sleep at about 12:30am. I woke up at about 2:00am to Levi's loud and labored breathing. We've been up ever since. We are pressing in (again) to the Lord. We are holding to Him and His promises. Our eyes are ever on the Lord for only He will release our feet from the snare. May we, in our deep valley, still gaze upon the beauty of the Lord and seek Him in his temple. We are still confident of this: We will see the goodness of the Lord in the land of the living. We will wait for the Lord, we will be strong and take heart and WAIT. I must confess in the waiting, I have become so weary and beaten down that I have had "words" with God. I felt, and told Him, that I was not pleased with the way He was handling this situation "I am ready Lord, I can't handle the waiting and the watching any longer, my limit has been reached,"come on Lord give us a break here!" "Lord, I'm calling to you...my back is against the wall and my face is against a "hard place." Save us! "Why is he getting worse?" Why would you give us the miracle of life but not finish it?" With each time I come to you Lord and he is not restored my faith becomes weaker and weaker, please sustain me, lift me up, hold me, I am desperate, so incredibly desperate for your touch... and then I read and seek Him in His word... *"The Lord shakes the desert, the voice of the Lord twists the oaks and strips the forests bare. And in His temple all cry, 'GLORY'"...The Lord gives strength to His people the Lord blesses His people with peace.* (Psalm 29:8-11). *"...I trust in the lord, I will be glad and rejoice in your love for you saw my affliction and knew the anguish of my soul, You have not handed me over to the enemy but have set my feet in a spacious place..."* (Psalm 31:7-8).

Levi is still breathing with extreme difficulty. His color is bad... the natural mind can't help but think the worst. But we choose to look with spiritual eyes. I have to pray with my eyes closed and NOT look at Levi because my natural mind will throw me into despair and hopelessness. We will still stand on the promise of LIFE. Stand with us please... We're claiming that the Son of Righteousness will rise with healing in his wings and Levi will get out and leap like a calf released from his stall... *"The Lord is doing a new thing now it springs up; do you not perceive it? He is making a way in the desert and streams in the wasteland..."* (Isaiah 43:19)

We are clinging to the Lord with white knuckles. Please come and cling with us for His name sake and for the Glory of the Lord to come to our Land like a Flood!!!!!!

~jami~

**December 20, 2001, 1 PM**

I am deeply saddened to announce that Levi took his last labored breath on earth at 1 o'clock today, surrounded once again by loving, faithful prayer warriors. He was never in any pain that we know of. Our prayers were answered, but not in the way we expected. God alone can answer all the questions that linger, and I'm sure will at some point. But one thing is certain: God is good, and what appears only evil and such a horrible loss now will somehow, someday be revealed as the incredible GOOD that the Lord intended all along. Ask Him to reveal the good He intends for you personally at this stage of the journey we have been travelling together with little Levi. After the testing comes the blessing. It's coming. Praise Jesus!

God bless us, every one,

Mel

# Levi's Legacy

It's funny, all my life, even as a little girl, I've had somewhat of a fixation with people who have continued to be "in love" with the Lord even in times of trauma. I wondered, "How does the Lord reveal himself in a time of deep pain? How does it feel? How does hope live? Is it really worth it?" And of course, the biggest question, "Why?"

I think of a story my friend Bill Jones told many years ago: There were two men in prison, waiting to be burned at the stake for their belief that Jesus is the Messiah... One man looked through the cell to the other man, Thomas Hauker, who would be executed in the morning. He said, "I need you to do me a favor, I need you to give me a sign that it is worth it to die for Christ. I need a sign that He is with you and does not leave you in your hour of deepest need." Mr. Hauker said, "Yes, I will do that for you. As I'm being burned, if it is worth it I will clap my hands together." The next day, he was tied to a stake and a fire was started at his feet. Mr. Hauker prayed for awhile, but fell silent as he grew weaker. His friend watched, waiting for "the sign". Mr. Hauker was still for a long while, and his friend thought he was dead. But suddenly, he raised his hands — now with no fingers and only melted flesh — over his head and joyfully clapped them three times as if in worship, signifying to all that Jesus had given him the strength to suffer for His name! IT WAS WORTH IT!!!!! (Phil. 3:7-10)

Now, I know that what we are experiencing is nothing like being burned at the stake (although my heart feels as if it is being burned at times), but I do feel the peace that passes all understanding. I do feel as if He is holding my hand through my darkest time.

*Have no fear, for I am with you; do not be looking about in trouble, for I am your God; I will give you strength, yes, I will be your helper; yes, my true right hand will be your support. For I, the Lord your God, have taken your right hand in mine, saying to you, Have no fear; I will be your helper.* Isaiah 41:10, 13 (Bible in Basic English)

A lot of people have said to me during this time, "Why would God allow this to happen to your family? You seem to have done everything 'right'." Well, I think I have an answer. It's all about purpose. Our purpose in life has become incredibly clear lately. In this country, we all think that life is all about being happy and avoiding all trauma. But that's not it. All of life is about becoming more and more conformed to the image of Christ no matter what you have to go through (Eph. 4:13-15).

I must admit that it sure was easy to go through the "godly" motions before all this came about, but He has shown Himself in such a deep and real way — a way that I would have never known before. He is with us and it is WORTH IT!!! It still hurts really bad but He is here. It's a funny thing about our Christian life... adversity and pain seem to grow us in ways that comfort and ease never can. Like a tree, our roots grow deep in search of His eternal water.

clay in His hands,

~jami~

In Loving Memory of

## *Levi*

David Levi Guinn
November 13, 1996 – December 20, 2001

Our "Little Man" of five years walked away from us
and into the strong and loving arms of His Heavenly Father.
When his battle began he was a frail little four year old.
But today after nine long months of fighting he is a mighty man.
He is a warrior that most grown men only dream of becoming.
The pain and anguish in our souls could never find expression.

We have many questions that cannot be answered right now
so we cling to what we DO know. And what we do know
is that God is still Good. He is the lover of our souls.
He is the Alpha and Omega, He is the Prince of Peace, He is the King of Kings…
and now He has a new name, "Levi's Playmate," a high and lofty position.

We used to sing together "Let Everything That Has Breath
Praise The Lord". Between each repetition of the words we would kiss
and then take a big breath… he no longer has breath as we know it.
But he has a "heavenly breath" and is undoubtedly praising the Lord with it.
We are still standing in awe of Jesus and will continuously go to Him for strength and sustenance…

*"One thing I ask of the Lord, this is what I seek;*
*that I may dwell in the house of the Lord all the days of my life,*
*to gaze upon the beauty of the Lord and seek Him in His temple.*
*For in the day of trouble He will keep me safe in His dwelling."*
Psalm 27:4, 5

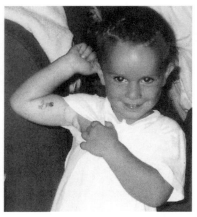

First tattoo...
'Toucan Sam' from the Fruit Loops box

Every man needs a special place for his "walkie-talkie"

Oh how we miss our chubby little man.
July 7th, Daddy's birthday.

Fishin' with the boys
...in Sky Valley, Ga. with our friends, the Carmichaels.

Backyard bathing with Dad ...before we knew what a blessing it was just to be together.

Graci feeding Levi. She was so glad it was finally her turn.
(December)

Mother's Day 2001 ...how was I to know that it would be my last with ALL my children with me.

Levi ...so proud of his new "ride"
(October)

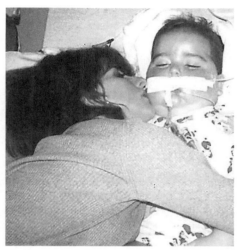

Levi scratching Mommy's back ...his love language.
(Thanksgiving Day)

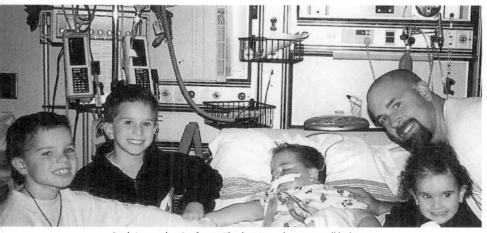

Just being together. Our favorite Thanksgiving ...because we still had Levi.

So refreshing!
(May)

The Three Amigos together again after treatment in Houston.
Jonah carried Levi's I.V. bag for him all day long. (September)

At Walt Disney World courtesy of Make A Wish Foundation.
Mickey and Minnie are great but where is Winnie the Pooh???? (June)

Reading all about it
...so what if it's upside down!

Sea World. When's nap time?

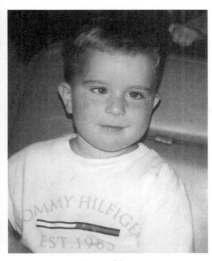

So peaceful…
he seemed to be doing so much better (July)

Sittin' with mommy in the shade.

Daddy and Levi at home about two weeks before he left us.

One of our first family photos without Levi — on top of Stone Mountain.

After...

# Levi's Legacy

## December 21, 2001

It's December 21st. I must say that yesterday was by far the the hardest day of my life ...Levi died.

I can't believe I just typed that... Levi died. How could that be. Will I live in excruciating pain all the days of my life? I feel destroyed and beaten beyond recognition. I am searching like never before for the word of the Lord to console me... "come quickly to my rescue; be my rock of refuge, a strong fortress to save me. Since you are my rock and my fortress for the sake of your name lead and guide me. Free me from the trap that is set for me"...

How did we get to this place?????????

All I know right now is that the visitation (viewing) will be at Tom M. Wages Funeral Home (3705 Hwy. 78 West, Snellville, GA 30078; 770-979-3200) between 5 and 7 PM Saturday Dec. 22nd, and the funeral will be at Lilburn Alliance Church (Hwy. 29 At Mimosa Drive, Lilburn, GA 30048; 770-921-1843) at 2:30 PM on Sunday.

Please pray for us. More than ever before we need a freshness from the Lord. We need His touch. He is doing a new thing... making a way in the desert and streams in the wasteland ...I will cling to that. But I do not understand His ways... Jeff is still my knight in shining armor, a pillar of strength for me to fall into ...Praise you Lord for him.

~jami~

## December 23, 2001

It's the end of the day, the funeral day. We have been totally surrounded with people all day. I am overwhelmed with the love and affirmation we received today...I feel so unworthy...

The Lord's grace has been so sufficient. I have felt lifted, held, even carried throughout this day.

But now we're home and tomorrow is Christmas Eve and I am having weird feelings. I can't explain it. It's sorrow and fear of the future but joy and relief all at the same time. I can't look at pictures of Levi yet. It's not the pictures of him when he was healthy that "get to me," it's the "last week" Levi pictures that cut my heart out. Oh Lord, I missed his healthy body for so long but now I feel foolish that I made a "fuss" about it when I would do anything just to have his chubby body here for just one more night, one more morning. I just want to tell him I love him one more time. I just want to touch him while he's still warm and soft. The longing in my heart is so deep, how could I put to words the depth of my pain? It's so deep that it's physical. I feel it in my whole body. My soul groans...but I don't let myself go "full force" into grieving, I cut myself off before I feel much. I'm so weary from pain. I'm numb. I'd rather not feel anything right now, just to get a reprieve from the agony that has become a part of me. Job, my new friend, a fellow "valley walker," said this: *"If only my anguish could be weighed and all my misery be placed on the scales it would surely outweigh the sand of the seas..."* (Job 6:2, 3) Oh how I bear witness with that, I feel that from within the deepest places of my soul. But with the same depth and intensity I feel – (Job 6:10) *"but let this be our one consolation...our joy in unrelenting pain...that we had not denied the words of the Holy One...Even now my witness is in heaven; my advocate is on high. My intercessor is my friend as my eyes pour out tears to God"* (16:19) ..."*But He knows the way that we take. When He has tested us; let us come forth as gold. Let our feet closely follow His steps: Let us keep to his ways without turning aside. Let us not depart from the commands of His lips; Let us treasure the words of His mouth more than our daily bread"* (23: 10-11). He is looking deep into my heart and Oh Lord, find good stuff ...be pleased...

Please "enter in" for us. I know it seems like it's all over. Levi is with Jesus ...Levi is safe, warm, forever "tucked in", victorious in his battle and his calling here on earth, he fought the good fight, he "finished well". But for me, the battle is just beginning. The road ahead is long and painful, I know because I feel the tip of it today. I know that if I let myself I could break into a million pieces right here in my chair, I am hanging on by a very thin thread. I sing praises to my Lord because I don't know what else to do.

I know that the eyes are the window to the soul so I look deep, deep, deep into the eyes of my children. I like to "lock on" and look at them. Not just a glance, not just look in the "eye" but the "soul" so that they know that I am sooooo interested in who they are, I want to know and love them in a spiritual way, a way that is deeper than average parents know each of their children.

I remember I used to just sit down and stare into Levi's eyes, I guess I knew that someday his eyes would not be here with me and soon the memory of them would be all I have. I see them now, in my mind and I miss them so terribly. Jesus, would you look into Levi's eyes for me, he'll know what you're doing. He'll know it's a "mommy thing". Would you run your hands through his floppy blonde hair, like I wish I could? Would you rub his hands and feet with oil like I long to do for him? Would you scratch his back for me? Oh Lord, my heart hurts so bad, will I ever heal?

~jami~

### Christmas Day, 2001

I know that it's kinda weird that I keep writing updates...I'm sorry – I just have to write out my feelings. I have to pour out the pieces of my heart on the computer screen and pick through the fragmented parts in search of anything that might be left. So far I don't find much other than unexplainable pain. (Words – they're more useless than ever. They are nothing but a slight drizzle in the ocean of expression)...

Last night was the most horrible night of my life. We had our family Christmas gathering. As I look at each one of my sweet, precious family I remember the special place each one of them held in Levi's heart. I could, in my minds eye, see every memory of them with my "little man." We covered over the pain with laughter and presents for the sake of the other children. But it was obvious. We are all a dam about to be broken, wondering what will be next in this wilderness journey through grief and sorrow.

My passion for life that used to be a fierce flame is now nothing more than a smoldering pile of rubble. I try to conjure up the desire but it's usually to no avail...

...I only filled three stockings last night...that was so sad. We were going to open Levi's presents this morning but I didn't feel strong enough so we put them all aside. I can't imagine that I will ever be at a place that I can actually look at them, open them. He loved to cook with me... we got him an easy bake oven, I know it's a girl thing but it was going to be my way of bringing the kitchen to him...I was so excited about seeing him open it. I can see him now...we bought him a robot, it was a really good one that had a remote control that he could make go and get things for him...we got a trampoline with the sides on it. We were looking forward to going out on it at night with sleeping bags and pillows and then listen to worship music, look up at the stars and talk about how cool God is for making them for us. (We used to do that on the back porch but it was gonna be extra cool on the trampoline...)

...I'm starting to have regrets...I'm remembering all the "mistakes" I made. I remember every time I got on to him when I was tired and couldn't be patient any longer... I see those eyes...their sadness...one time he was sitting at the bar stool in the kitchen, he had been there for hours eating...finally I said (with agitation that he was constantly eating...) "okay, let's go into the den"...he looked at me and said, "but wait, I wanted to ask you a question...through tears he said, "I was just wondering if I could have dessert... holding his finger and thumb closely together to signify "a little bit", "just a tiny little bit?" I felt so bad for making him feel guilty for being hungry, I fell down on my knees and put my head into his lap and cried like a baby. He stroked my hair with his one good arm and cried with me. He cried so hard... And then , he turned my face up to look at his and he said, "Will you forgive me, Mommy?"...sweet, sweet, sweet little man of mine...how will I live without you here? Oh Lord, I never knew that sorrow was so deep and cruel with tentacles that have no rhyme or reason. Who knows where my mind will take me next...Lord, help me to tuck it away for now...my other children need me to be happy today. Give me strength. Please radiate your joy through me, somehow, someway, I don't know how you will do it. But, I'll just have to leave it up to you...I trust in You Lord, You have never forsaken me. But it has never been harder to rejoice in You. Help me... Jesus, tell Levi 'Merry Christmas' from us!

~jami~


**December 27, 2001**

The days are harder and longer than ever... Last night we rented a movie and just "vegged out" but even that is different now. First of all, movies are soooo senseless now. It's almost as if the movie makers in Hollywood just think of any old subject and go with it. Just a waste of time, a waste of good, sweet, precious, forever gone time...Second of all, we were (unwisely) trying to "lose" ourselves in someone else's life to take a break from the constant grief. The only thing we forgot to think about is that the movie had to end sometime...when the movie ended we were thrown back into the painful reality that Levi is not with us. The movie we were watching was about World War 2 and all its atrocities but it seemed easier than the reality that is now ours... I couldn't stop crying, I couldn't sleep, I just laid in bed and stared at the moonlight shining through the cracks of the blinds. I used to do that before Levi "left" and would wonder what it would be like if/when he wasn't here...it's much worse than I ever could have imagined...how could we have known how it would feel to live out our nightmare?

Levi has been with Jesus for one week today. It's funny how eternity used to be something we hoped for but would understand "later" and we kept it that way as if savoring a surprise. I just never investigated heaven and what scripture says about it. I kinda felt like "there will be time for celebrating later but today we must focus on the 'work at hand.'"... Now that Levi is a resident there I can't learn enough about it. I search, dig, and scrape the scriptures to learn more about Levi's new home. I pray for wisdom, visions, revelations... anything that will help me to "see" him in his comfort...before Levi went there, only one corner of my heart was focused on the things of eternity, but now, only one corner of my heart is here...we have a stored up "treasure" there and we can't wait to get back to him. We almost rear-ended a car yesterday, Jeff was in "another world" and had to slam on the breaks to keep from ramming the guy in front of us. No one was even scared. Out of the silence Caleb said, "Wow, we almost went to be with Levi, that would have been so cool."... at bath time last night Graci said, "I miss Levi and I just want to go to heaven to be with him." (It's so hard to see her playing by herself, they were so inseparable...and now she's without a playmate.) Overtime Jonah prays he wants Jesus to say "Hi" to Levi... "and tell him we miss him so bad down here."

I can't believe that my "little man" is somewhere I have never been before. It's so strange...I am such a control freak with my children. I know everything they eat, drink, wear, see, learn, read... I even know what they're thinking. But now, I know none of that about Levi. I almost feel irresponsible. Isn't that crazy? Our family feels so incomplete now. I long for that completeness. I feel so lost without all four of my children to take care of.

I know that out of the ashes, the rubble and the cold hard ground come beauty, hope and roses. But I'm still in the "rubble stage" wondering how I will ever move on... I wonder if he knew how much I love him, how could he" I didn't even know. I hope that somewhere along the way in my foolish and imperfect mothering, my heart spoke to his heart –in a way that words, tears, hugs and kisses could never express...

...but the Lord did not leave me empty handed. I have Caleb, Jonah and Graci... sometimes I hold them close and cry silently. I scratch their backs and hug them, I hold them, rub their feet... I even imagine that I am doing this to Levi. I rubbed Graci's feet last night and it was sooo much like Levi was still here. I miss his feet. I miss his chubby hands. I miss his crossed eyes, Whenever I imagine his face it's not long before the face that I see is the face that was in the casket. I hate that...I want my mind to stay on his "alive face." I am broken.

The sacrifices of God are a broken spirit; a broken and contrite heart, O God, you will not despise. (Psalm 51:17) I pray that my heart is honorable to the Lord. That my brokenness will be a sweet gift to the Him.

Record my lament, list my tears on your scroll – are they not in your record? Psalm 56:8

Oh Lord, give me the strength to do well with what I have been given. Create in me a pure heart. It feels so empty right now, surely you will fill it with purpose and purity. Surely this pain will not be without great purpose. Surely…it feels so useless right now. It seems like such a bad plan. Don't you know that I am too weak for this? Don't you know that I am not a warrior? I am a child… I can't live without him here. But I have to. Oh Lord, be my strength. I feel so lost, weak, useless, sad…Help me Jesus to set my face like flint before you, to stand.

## January 2, 2002

*"For the Lord is Good and His love endures forever, He's a faithful God to all generations For the Lord is Good and His mercies will not Fail us, they are new each day. Lift your voice and say The Lord is Good!" I lift my eyes to the hills for where does my help come from? My help comes from the Lord who made heaven and earth. The Lord is my keeper the shade on my right hand. The Lord is my keeper from this time forth and forever more…* I find myself constantly saying words like these. They are the only light on my path these days. I am at a point that I have never been. I feel myself questioning the Lord. I feel myself wondering if He really loves me. The pain in my heart can do nothing but question. Lord, do I trust you? What are you doing? I am racked with pain…In my earthly way of thinking love is not so hard. Love "feels" better than this…so now more than ever I am pushed to ponder the "ways" of God. I am at a place of seeing how helplessly dependent I am on Him. There's no way I could have truly understood that before… You just don't "get it" until you watch your child take his last breath and there you are just watching. His body is lifeless and losing its color before your eyes and what do you do? NOTHING!!!!!!!!!! You know why you do nothing? Because it's all you can do… What a rude awakening to how ridiculously weak we are as human beings… worthless… I am nothing… My heart grows restless in my search for significance in this pain and loss… It's a strange "brotherhood" the bond between sorrow and joy… The loss and the hand of God finding my life worthy of such "pressing," molding, changing. But I find that I am a creature of habit and the habit I had formed was one of comfort and even a "health and wealth" theology. What happened? Yesterday the sky was blue and clear, faith flowed like a river and today the sky is gray and unclear my faith is thin and breakable… Stephen Curtis Chapman sings a song that "works" for me these days…"Pain falls like a curtain on the things I once called certain and I have to say the words I fear the most…"I just don't know" and the questions without answers come and paralyze the dancer (us) so I stand here on the stage (that is life) afraid to move, afraid to fall. Oh, but fall I must…on this truth that my life has been formed from the dust… God is God and I AM NOT…I can only see a part of the picture He's painting… He is great and Holy and I will cling to that.

Edwin Markham said this: "Defeat may serve as well as victory to shake the soul and let the glory out. When the great oak is straining in the wind, the boughs drink in new beauty, and the trunk sends down a deeper root on the windward side. Only the soul that knows the mighty grief can know the mighty rapture. Sorrow comes to stretch out spaces in the heart for joy." In other words without hard times and pressing, even times of near defeat we stagnate and die… "no greater failure can there be than to waste the daily opportunities God grants us. Opportunities which, once squandered, can never be retrieved. God gives only today, this hour, this moment"… "The clock of life is wound but once and no man has the power to tell just when the hand will stop on what day – or what hour. Now is the only time you have so live it with will. Don't wait until tomorrow, the hands may then be still." (Author unknown)…Even as I type these words I feel incredibly fragile so don't think for one moment that I am strong… I am weak and on the verge of crumbling. As a matter of fact, I never knew that a person could be this close to destruction without actually dissolving. If it weren't for family and friends I think I would die of a broken heart. I guess that's right where the Lord wants me. But I must say that this is the last place I want to be…I am clay…dull, lifeless clay, waiting to see what beauty could possibly come out of me…

~jami~


**January 6, 2002**

It's a rainy Sunday morning. I woke up at 4:00am with that "hollow" feeling. Weather affects me in big ways now. Because now I think about Levi's grave site and how cold and lonely it is there. I haven't been there since he was buried but I can see it in my mind very clearly. I know his spirit is not there but I am still confined to seeing him in the body that he had while he was here. It's all I've ever known, it's the "shell" that I fought to keep but lost, sometimes I wish I could have just kept his body here at home so I could hold what's left of him here on earth… I'm desperate to "feel" him. To touch him…

Levi had been asking since June, "When is it gonna snow again?" so the snow this year was really hard. I kept wishing I could dress him in the "layers" like I usually do when it snows. You know, 4 shirts, 2 pairs of pants, 3 pair of socks, boots, a big jacket, hats, gloves… the whole nine yards. Preparing for 30 minutes to make the yearly snow man…then five minutes after they all get out there they come back in throw all their wet clothes on the floor in front of the door, run to sit in front of the fireplace and say, "wow, that was fun but it sure is cold out there"… He used to get so excited about the smallest things. I miss that. I miss his goofy little run, the way he threw his head back when he laughed, the way he played with Caleb, Jonah and Graci. I would give ALL I own to see his face laugh just one more time…

…today it's raining and I remember how he loved the rain. In the Summer when a big rain would start he would beg me to go out and run in the rain, play in the puddles. All our neighbors would come out and watch as all our kids would just "go crazy" together in the rain. It had kinda become a ritual. What a sweet memory. What a painful realization that I will never see Levi play in the rain again (here). I wonder if there's rain in heaven????

# Levi's Legacy

...I now have a "Levi box". It's a box of pictures, his green corduroy golf hat, a T-shirt that he wore the day before he died (it still has carrot apple juice that he spilled on it), the anointing oil that I can smell that immediately brings my mind to see him. I also have a dirty towel that he used the day before he died. It still smells like him (I will never, never wash it). I also have a pair of his little boxer shorts in there, they're so cute and small... and his broviac, the line to the main artery in his heart (that sweet little heart that I learned to appreciate each beat of...) that they took off of his body before they put him in the casket. So, now when I miss him really bad and I just need to remember I take my box and cherish every memory, thought, smell...It hurts so bad but I can't "not remember" does that make sense? I have an "incurable wound" and I'm just trying to get used to living with it.

One battle I am fighting now (along with many others) is learning to be grateful for five (too short) years with Levi instead of being angry for not getting the usual 60 plus years that we think is a guarantee.

But the biggest battle that I have rocking my existence right now is the lack of Gods presence. During the funeral I felt carried by the Father. I was okay. But the day after the funeral I felt as if the spirit of the Lord left me... I have been angry at the Lord for this. "How could you leave me when I need you the most?" "I need to 'feel' you here with me and you're nowhere to be found"... But I'm learning... In Philippians 3:10 it says, *"I want to know Christ and the power of his resurrection and the fellowship of sharing in His sufferings, becoming like Him in his death"...* There you have it! When Christ was crucified He said *"My God, My God, why have you forsaken me?"* I feel that "forsaken" thing. (Not that my anguish can come remotely close to what Christ endured on the cross, He has shown me one corner of it) It's almost as if the Lord has allowed me to feel the empty, separated, abandoned despair that is hell so that I would be more passionate for the "lost." So that I would not be hesitant to speak the truth about the ways of salvation. How could I hold back the truth of His Love when I have felt the rejections, loneliness and eternal longings that there are in hell?

In my disappointed hope I have been forced to look at God in a new way. All the "feel good" stuff is useless. I have to ask myself with more sincerity than ever before, "Do I really believe that God will do as he says? Can I truly hope in the Lord? "You never know what you believe until it's a matter of life and death"... (C. S. Lewis) Can I "wait" on Him? The word "wait" in Isaiah 40:31 means "to literally bind together by twisting." Hope is waiting, and anticipating God's promises being fulfilled and while we wait we are binding, twisting, braiding together, becoming one with God... I am still living in the "dark night of my soul" but I know He has not forsaken me. It's just different now. I am forced into "naked faith," (faith that doesn't depend upon feelings.) It's a totally new concept for me. And I must say that I do not agree with God's timing on this. I think it would be best if He lavished His presence on me. But as I already know His ways are not ours...some day I will see clearly that this way is best. But today I am forced to trust Him at a new level. I just keep reminding myself that..."He is using sorrow to stretch out a bigger place for joy to come in later"... and..."He who cannot endure the 'bad' will not live to see the 'good'" (Yiddish proverb). So, I'm just living. That's all, nothing more. Just waiting to see the "good" that I am confident the Lord is bringing. Lord, help me to be strong and of good courage, I desperately search for your faint whisper. I say along with Job, *"Though you slay me, yet will I trust you..."* (Job 13:15)

"The bottom line is, the further removed our faith is from resting on our feelings and our sight, the closer we are to true faith in God." (Chuck and Nancy Missler)

I must admit I don't like all this "non-feeling" stuff but I guess I'm not supposed to...please pray for us we need it more than ever. And please don't stop writing... Sometimes the encouragement that comes over the Internet and through the mail is what helps us get out of bed in the morning. Your words of love and wisdom are priceless to us. I truly believe that He personifies His arms of love through each of you. Someone asked me the other day, "Do you actually read all of those e-mails and letters you get?"... my response: "Are you kiddin'? I savor each one of them. When we come home from being out someplace Jeff and I almost race to the computer to see if anyone wrote (even if it's just someone saying, "I don't know what to say." We feel linked in arms because we are confused too!) When I go down to have my quiet time I can't wait to see what God is doing in the lives of others, it gives purpose to our pain. You could never know how Christ's love is poured out on us through your thoughts, prayers and writings. Thank you, Thank you, Thank you...

~jami~


**January 8, 2002**

Jeff has lots of incredible gifts ...expressing the plethora of goodness in his heart is not one of them (I say that not as an insult but as a compliment because I underestimate how precious his heart is because he can't show the treasure hidden within). Every time he tries to put to words his feelings he is left unsatisfied with what comes out. But the other day we were talking about how we feel and trying to "get out" the pain trapped within. This is what he said: "You know in the movie 'It's A Wonderful Life' when George came home and his little girl, Zuzu was sick in bed? And remember when she showed her daddy her flower? And then the pedals of the flower broke and fell off? Do you remember what she said to her daddy?" ...She said so simply, so beautifully, "Daddy, please fix it, please fix my flower!" Through tears Jeff said, "That's how I feel." The psalmist couldn't have said it better. That's it! That sums it all up. Oh Daddy God, Please fix our flower!"

Right now in this part (I hate words like 'phase' or 'process'; they make me feel like a machine and not a person) of the journey the fight for the day is the "battle of the longings." My longing is for Levi. I look at pictures and desperation to touch him comes over me. It is the deepest desire I have ever felt in my life. It takes me over like a flood and it is left unfulfilled. I touch his empty clothes and try so hard to remember what he felt like in those clothes. I remember every time I put his little man underwear on ...with all four of them... I would get them out of the tub and put their underwear on and they would run because they would know that I was about to squeeze their little bottoms and say "Cutie patootie!" I know that sounds so goofy but it's what I did. I miss that! I miss him running and acting like he was trying to get away from me but loving it when I would catch him, hug him, squeeze him. Have I ever wanted anything more than I want to hold him now?...

...I remember how Jesus met all of our needs and longings as we walked through the nightmare of the brain tumor. At that time it was the "longing" of my heart to know Him more intimately. To know Him as fully as possible this side of heaven. I knew I would never make it if I didn't pursue Him and His ways (and as always He pursued me more than I pursued Him) But now Levi is on the "other side" and I miss him... I miss him, I miss him, I miss him!!! ... And the truth is that my longing for Levi seems to be greater than my longing for the Lord. I guess what I really want is for things to be the way they used to be. And I am comforted to know that Job felt the same way...He said: *"How I long for the months gone by, for the days when God watched over me. Oh, for the days when I was in my prime, when God's intimate friendship blessed my house, when the Almighty was still with me and my children (all of them) were around me."* (Job 29:2,4,5). I know the Lord is here. I know a little more each day that He never left me. But, oh how I miss the "good ol' days." The days when I could have it "all." But I can't. The other day I overheard Graci and Sydney (my niece) playing. Out of the blue Sydney said, "I wish Levi didn't die." (Sydney's heart is so tender) and Graci (who is a little more brash) responded by saying, "but he did Syd." How can she be only three years old and so keen to the hard facts of life. [Maybe because she dreams about Levi almost every night. She is "rejuvenated" each night by play time with Levi, in her dreams. (I am jealously waiting for my dream)]... I remember all the times that I have told my kids, "Life is hard and it only gets harder as you get older"... I guess she's been listening a little too intently...

Oh Lord, life IS hard and even cruel at times. But you are not. You are kind and loving. Please give me the strength and wisdom to separate the two. I never expected life to be easy. We knew the day we chose to follow You that we would endure incredible hardships. We knew that Satan would "go for" our children. We knew it!!!! We knew that we would never be the "all American" family in pursuit of the "all American" dream because Satan was "on us" trying to push us to the point of cursing God and giving up!!! Help us to put it "in his face" that we stand on truth. We will not cower under pressure!! (only because You give us the strength). We will "rejoice though now for a little while we have had to suffer grief in all kinds of trials. These have come so that our faith — of greater worth than gold which perishes even though refined by fire — may be proved genuine and may result in praise, glory and honor when Jesus Christ is revealed" (1 Peter 1:6,7) (I've always loved those verses...but now they are written in the blood that flows from my broken heart.) Oh Father, restore us. Make us strong, firm and steadfast. Sweep this distance away, hold me close to your face. Help us to *"be careful, and watch ourselves closely so that we do not forget the things our eyes have seen or let them slip from our hearts as long as we live. We will commit to teach them to our children and to their children after them..."* (Deut. 4:9)

Amen

**January 11, 2002**

RANDOM THOUGHTS...

As I walk through my new life of learning to live without Levi I am much more sensitive to "never again moments" I didn't notice until I had lost my chance to make moments. My time is "up." I have had my last moments with my "little man." I will never again be given the opportunity to pull over on the side of a busy road just because he needed a hug. I will never get to say, "Hey, ya want to go get an ice cream cone, just you and me?" (but surely there's ice cream in heaven?????) I will never get to sing him songs and tuck him in at night. I will never again go in the bathroom after him and have to wipe the toilet seat and turn the light off because he forgot (and I used to complain)... never again... I've developed the last roll of film with him in the pictures. I've washed his last load of dirty clothes. I've made his bed for the last time, I'll never hear him say, "hey, my tooth fell out!!!!!!" (He was so looking forward to losing his teeth like his big brothers) . I'll never cut his hair again. I'll never put sunscreen on him at the pool. I'll never cut his fingernails and toenails, I'll never clean his ears ( he used to bring me Q-tips and lay his head on my lap, he never said a word, he never had to) I'll never give him a bath and I'll never scratch his back...and there are a million more "nevers". Everything is different now. No matter what I do I'm wondering, have I done this since Levi left?

The day I gave birth to Caleb I began to dream big dreams for him. Then Jonah, then Levi, then Graci. It's what a mom does, she dreams for her children. How do I stop? All through the day I think of a million different thoughts and wonderings about each of them. How do I cut it off for him? I know that all his dreams are completed in heaven but what do I do about my way of thinking here and now? I know I will learn but I kinda don't want to. I like dreaming for him. I like seeing him as a man (in my mind) I like to envision our family picture in 10 years with him in it. I have prayed for all my children's spouses since they were born. What will become of Levi's wife? There's some girl out there who will never know what she missed. I know that God doesn't make mistakes. His plans are not thwarted. If Levi is not alive today it's because God never intended him to live past five years old. I find comfort in that... but my mind is a little slow on those kinds of things. I can't just turn my way of thinking off. I have to re-learn. And I'm a slow learner...

Here's a cool thought: Levi was my only C-section. And I have always hated that scar. Not that anyone would ever notice it "but I did and it feels funny and it kinda pokes out in an ugly way"... that was before ...now it's my badge of honor. It's"the mark" that God gave. It's a sweet keepsake that will be with me for as long as I live in this body. I think that's cool that God knew five years ago that I would someday love this old scar, even need it. It was a gift disguised. Thank you Jesus. You are good.

I hang tightly to this verse: *"There is hope for a tree, if it is cut down, it will sprout again"*...Job 14:7. Someday I will see its truth more clearly, but for now I just hold onto it waiting for the day when life truly grows in the place in my heart reserved just for Levi... I will never completely heal — I know that in some ways I will grieve my loss of him for the rest of my life. I trust that Jesus will walk me through that, one day at a time using it to increase my desire to see His Kingdom come and Levi along with it.

Sometimes I wonder if a day will ever go by that I don't cry. I've noticed that since Levi has gone I cry differently. There are more tears. Not only because I cry more but literally, more tears come out and they're big tears. It's really strange. Surely the Lord does "bottle" each tear... "There is a sacredness in tears. They are not the mark of weakness, but of power. They speak more eloquently than 10,000 tongues. They are the messengers of overwhelming grief, of deep contrition and of unspeakable love." (Washington Irving) I wince when I read the part in that quote about power because that's the last thing I feel in myself. It's His power, NOT mine. I've never felt weaker than I do right now...

~jami~

p.s. I went to the grave site yesterday. It was the first time since we buried him. I had a friend with me but if I had been alone I could have easily fallen apart. It was strange. There's no headstone yet so you can hardly tell where his body is. I was looking around at all the other grave sites...they all had these beautiful headstones, flowers, notes... I almost felt like maybe Levi felt unloved because he didn't have anything on his grave site. I thought to myself, "We've got to get some "stuff" out here so everyone will know how much we love him." Is that the most ridiculous thing you've ever heard of? What's wrong with me?


## January 12, 2002

WHAT IS A MAN? A "REAL" MAN?

In my years of living as a woman I've come up with some staunch thoughts on what a real man is. When I was a little girl I thought of a man as someone who had facial hair. (That was true in some cases.) But now after many years of silently watching the world and the definition of a man that has been so carelessly created through weakness and ignorance I have come up with my own definition, my own ideas. The world says that a man is "strong" so he doesn't cry or show any sign of tenderness. But to me a "real" man cries. He is not afraid to show the passions in his heart. He is not a coward hiding behind the lie that he is too strong to break. A "real" man is transparent with his weaknesses. Only the bravest of men actually talk openly about the fears and shortcomings of their character. The world says that success is determined by the amount of money he makes and the size of his house , the number of "toys" he accumulated in his lifetime, the amount of money he has hidden in his safe. But I dare say that those who hold so tightly to the things of this world are fools. And I can say that because the Lord said it! "What does it profit a man if he gains the whole world and loses his soul?" It doesn't take a rocket scientist to see that "stuff" will lose its value and can be forever lost, ruined. But the soul of a human goes on without end. A "real" man would give away all he owns to be with his family and friends if he had to. A real man stays home from work because his wife just needs to be with him. A real man listens...and then, (if needed) he talks...a real man "falls" and then gets back up. A real man knows that success has nothing to do with money and things but everything to do with people, love and the pursuit of becoming the man God has intended him to be.

A "real" man loves Jesus and clings to his word desperately searching for the guidance that is there to lead his family. A "real" man "eats quiche" because he doesn't worry about what others think, his mind and heart are fully surrendered to the Lord. He performs to an audience of ONE. He serves his wife and children instead of expecting to be served. He doesn't keep a record of all the shortcomings of his loved ones. He hardly ever notices others' weaknesses because he's too busy checking out his own. A real man tells his wife she's beautiful everyday even though the signs of aging are rapidly changing her looks (sometimes she looks in the mirror and says "who's that old lady and where's the beautiful girl my husband always talks about?"). A real man is burdened for his children's future. A real man changes poopie diapers. A real man does dishes and laundry. A real man disciplines his children knowing that it will save their souls in the end. A real man has bad days. A real man pursues his children and the hidden treasure that lies deep within their hearts. A real man prays face down. A real man is constantly making sacrifices for his family. A real man makes the road rise up to meet his wife…You know how I know what a real man is? I'm married to one.

[next day… As I read over my observations of a "real man" I realize that I could have made a big mistake by making others feel inadequate. I was just playing around with my thoughts toward Jeff and how he has been a shining example of a godly man. But when I saw it on the web page I thought of my dad, my brothers (David and Dicky), Chris (my brother-in-law) and Mel, all of which I consider incredible men who have impacted my life by their character and love. In no way did I intend to make any other man feel unworthy to be called a "real man." It might not be necessary to say this but I have to, for my own peace of mind. Let the record show that I, in my lifetime have had the rare blessing of being loved, respected and even cherished by some pretty incredible men who have in turn helped me to see that "The Man of all Men" (my Heavenly Father) is loving, true, compassionate and gentle…]

## January 14, 2002

A Memory to Share…

My mom has kept a journal for as long as I can remember… I learned from her that time goes by quickly and our minds can't keep up with all the great things that the Lord does so it's a good idea to write it down… She never actually told me that I just watched her…she was looking back in her journals and enjoying the happenings of Levi and told me about this special moment…One afternoon PaPa (my dad) took Caleb and Jonah to burger king. When Levi found out about this unwise decision on PaPa's part he reprimanded him saying that "burger king is not a good place for our family to eat, it's bad for you!!! Later on that day we were leaving to go home and everyone was piling into the car. Levi was getting in the car and had a quick change of heart. He turned around and ran back into the house. He had rethought the "chastening" he had given PaPa and didn't want him to feel bad) so he found him and said, "PaPa, I love you and I like you too." he then turned and ran back to get in the car…sweet, sweet little man, how did you get to be such a kind, thoughtful, tender little man?

Anyway...I figured since you have joined us in our grief you should have the pleasure of knowing the memories too!!!!!

## January 17, 2002

I look outside at the trees and the grass, the leaves left over from the Fall...they're all still, completely still, there's no wind, no rain, no movement. That's strange to me. How can the world around me be so calm and still when there's a storm raging in my soul right now... I think it's a control issue. I am mourning the loss of (the sense of) control in my life. I have spun and am spinning. I feel useless and totally without power. How could we have let him slip through our fingers, he was here and now he's not, we dropped him, we lost him...the trees and the wind have learned something that I haven't grasped yet. Surrender. I feel the need for control, I want some "say-so", some part in the final decision, I want my life back, I want the hope of healing, I want Levi back...

Yesterday we were driving down the road listening to praise music...suddenly out of the back seat Graci said, "he just ran away," I was shocked, I turned around and said, "who?" she never looked up, she just said, "Levi... he just ran away." My heart sank; it was broken for her loss and lack of understanding. "Oh no, sweetie he had to go, the body he had here was broken so he had to go and get another one that works better." She quickly came back with, "Nope, he just didn't want me anymore." I started to have a feeling of panic in my heart, I wanted to help her to understand. So, quickly I came back with, "No, no, no, Levi loves you so much, you are so special to him!!!", but she wasted no time, she knew exactly how she felt about this. She said, "If he loved me he'd come back to me"... I was defeated in my struggle to comfort her. I continued to tell her that Levi loved her and didn't choose to leave her but the expression on her face told me that she was sticking with the "actions speak louder than words" thing that I've always told her...

Oh Lord, what do I do with that? What do I say? How do I comfort when I am drowning in sorrow myself? I'm not only out of control of my life, I'm out of control of my children's lives too... God, why didn't you heal Levi? You say that if we have the faith of a mustard seed we can move mountains...surely we had that much faith...why didn't you move our mountain??? I don't understand...we prayed, we battled, we prayed and prayed and prayed...help me to rest in Your presence, help me to sit still, accept this burden, receive what you have entrusted to us. I want to be more like you Jesus, but joining You in Your suffering – I never fully understood what that entailed (and still don't). But as far as I can see right now, it means surrender. That used to sound so easy. But that was before it meant sacrificing my son. When C.S. Lewis' wife was sick and dying of cancer his priest/pastor said, "It's good that you have faith and pray. That will help you get through this." Lewis responded, "I pray because I don't know what else to do, I pray because I'm desperate. It doesn't change God, IT CHANGES ME." That's the bottom line, isn't it? I'm not going to change God's mind, but He's going to change my heart. Once again, sounds so easy...it's not...

I think it would be a little more tolerable if I could feel Him, sense His presence. I can't. I know He is here, I know He is right by my side, but it's a vague feeling. It's right there just one step before the abandonment feeling...so I ransack the scriptures for understanding, for some word that will help me to KNOW Him and His ways a little better...*"Give ear to my words, O Lord, consider my sighing. Listen to my cry for help, my King and my God, for to you I pray. In the morning, O Lord, you hear my voice; in the morning I lay my requests before you and wait in expectation..."* (Psalm 5:1,2)

I'm waiting...my hope is in You, show me your ways, guide me in truth...~jami~


**January 23, 2002**

It's raining...again. I woke up thinking about Levi's grave site...again. Cold, lonely, wet. I wish I could get over that. I have to keep saying to myself, "he's not there, he's not there, he's not there..."

Sometimes I think I'm starting to heal. I think I will have a "normal" day, a day without crying. But then the grief, the sorrow will sneak up behind and choke me. It's a strange feeling, it starts in the center of my body and then shoots out to the rest of my body and leaves my hair standing on end. I never knew that grief was something you felt physically. I am learning that I can choose whether or not I will drown in my deep sadness or reach to Christ for help, encouragement, purpose. I am still going through a time of numbness. I can't really feel anything except pain, and that, I feel quite completely. The only time I can "feel" is when I worship. The Lord really has me 'over a barrel' because at times the last thing I want to do is praise Him but if I want to "feel" alive I have to. When Levi was so close to death and breathing with such difficulty, I knew (as much as I could grasp it) that he would die soon if the Lord didn't heal him really quickly. I was on my knees next to him on the bed and the scripture that came to mind was in Job 13:15: *"Though You slay me , yet will I praise You."* I just kept saying it over and over again. Now, before you think,"Wow, she's so spiritual," let me tell you this: I think if I were to search the motives of my heart I would find that I was manipulating God. As if to say "Look, I'm praising you at my darkest hour so wouldn't it be appropriate for you step in and heal him to reward me for my faithfulness?" But the bummer is that you can't manipulate someone who knows your heart better than you do...

When Jeff and I got married we were planning to go overseas and be full-time missionaries, but we had babies really quickly (got pregnant 5 weeks after we were married) so we waited for the Lord's direction. After seeking and praying we knew the Lord was calling us to be "missionaries" to our children... a long time ago missionaries would pack all their belongings in a coffin, knowing that they would probably be killed. Their friends and family would come to see them off and say, "how foolish to go away knowing that you will die." Their response was, "Oh no, we've already died." ...of course insinuating that they had died to themselves to live for Christ. So, with that in mind I am brought to these questions, "Did I die, or am I dying?" "Will I be soft clay on the potter's wheel or will I allow myself to become cold and hard, unmoldable?" Why waste Levi's life and death? We've come this far, so come on Lord, take my hand and let's push on through...but it's gonna have to be ALL you, Lord. I am worthless, fearful, wimpy…damaged goods. The only thing I have going for me is desperation for You to "use" me to the fullest. Lord, would you fill me, heal me, change me, give me the grace to receive Your "call"? Most of all would you help me to live with the mindset that Levi is not in my past, he's in my future? I think I can make it if I look at it that way…Charles F. Kettering said: "We should all be concerned about the future (heaven in this case) because we will have to spend the rest of our lives there." I can't wait!!

~jami~

## January 25, 2002

I woke up sad today… missing Levi, wondering what he's doing right now. I woke up wishing I could hold him just one more time. I imagined holding his chubby body, our faces cheek to cheek. I remember thinking every time I held him, "I wonder how much longer I get to do this? I wonder if I'll be able to remember what he feels like"… I imagined what it was like to have him, the "trouble of him," I would get up in the morning go down stairs and have time with the Lord, seeking the scriptures, inviting the Holy Spirit to come… to show me how to allow the spirit of Christ to live in me…to love Jeff and my children through me. How else could I love them properly? Next, I would get on the treadmill and run, pray, think…a million different thoughts. I would have to have a pencil and paper close by so that I could jot down some of the things swimming around in my mind…when Levi woke up I would then go upstairs and begin "the process." Oh, how I miss it!!! How could I have ever complained? What a fool!!! I'd get all the medicine together and give them in the right order. He knew the schedule. The antioxidant powder first. After that he would (every single morning) point to the tub. He was right—it was "time." I would pick up his sweet, 70 lb. body, limp and unable to help. I would take him to the tub and sit him up just right so he could sit up without falling. He would remind me of the next step of the day: the carrot apple juice, I would go make it and get "the" straw. They (Graci and Levi) would drink their juice and talk and play for sometimes an hour. That was their special time together (Graci has "tub crayons" and draws Levi there now). It breaks my heart to see her "playing" with and talking to the stick man drawn on the wall of the tub. We miss him so much. We miss our routine with him in it…the routine would go on every day almost identical to the day before. How I miss the sameness that I once complained about…

I don't always let myself "go there" but today I indulged myself for just a little while. but now I have to retrieve my heart. I have to force myself to see today. To live in the now. I admit it is so hard because Levi is not here in today. He is in yesterday. How does one live this way? How does one learn to look forward? I long for understanding in this drama that has unfolded in our lives. But in the last month I have seen that I might never have that. So, I am left to trust the Lord without it. He never said we would understand. Did Joseph understand why his brothers sold him into slavery? Did Moses understand why he was suddenly living in the desert when he was a prince in Egypt the day before? Did Job understand why his whole family was killed and all he owned destroyed? Surely they were as "shocked" as we are. Surely they had a million questions and a longing for some explanation just like we do. But that's just too bad—they didn't get one and neither will we. Not right now anyway... I love what Job said when his wife said, *"Are you still hanging on to your integrity? Curse God and die!"* Job said this: *"You are talking like a foolish woman. Shall we accept good from God, and not trouble?"* Wow, he really had a grip on what it meant to trust God in the darkness without understanding. (But I do wonder if he thought, "God, why didn't you take her too, she's getting on my nerves? I know Jeff has thought the same about me...) I have praised God in the light of His blessings. Now, I must learn to praise Him in the darkness. I remember being on a mission trip in Dominican Republic (15 years ago). We were worshipping in an old church with no windows, it was about 105 degrees, the mosquitoes were eating me alive... I was thinking to myself, "I am so uncomfortable I can't worship. I can't focus on the Lord because I am so frustrated with these lousy circumstances... then I looked at the old woman next to me. She was barefoot, her toes were mangled and ugly from years of working in the fields, there were flies around the open wounds. She had an old dirty dress hanging on her very thin frame. As my eyes moved up from her feet to her hands I was put to shame... she was passionately praising her God with broken and overworked hands, raised as an offering, tears streaming down her cheeks with adoration for the Lord... I admired her. I knew I could only dream of becoming a woman of such character and obedience. Now, is my chance to praise Him in my brokenness. May He give me the strength to be a fraction of the woman I saw that day.

I am trusting Jesus to make this tragedy into something beautiful beyond imagination... *"He has made everything beautiful in its time. He has also set eternity in the hearts of men, yet they cannot fathom what God has done from the beginning to end."* Ecclesiastes 3:11. Oh Lord, let it be... may Your beauty be revealed in us. May your plan be fulfilled in us. "May we not despise or oppose what we do not understand." (William Penn)

~jami~

### January 29, 2002

Yesterday Jeff came home from running some errands. He had gone by the funeral home to talk to them about Levi's tombstone. He walked past the room where Levi's "viewing" was. There was a casket in the same place that Levi's was. Jeff said he felt drawn in... he went closer and closer. It was an older woman. "She looked beautiful, she was about 85 years old but she had the most beautiful and peaceful look on her face." It was a weird experience. Once again, death had taken someone. This time it was someone's mom, wife, grandmother, maybe great-grandmother. Death, how cruel you are, how much I despise you. But you know what? We all have to face it. We're all gonna die. We've always known that of course, but now it's different. We had to walk Levi right up to it and then let go. We could go no further, he had to go alone. Isn't that a bizarre thought? Jeff and I taught him everything. We taught him how to walk, talk, dress, brush his teeth... but we never taught him how to die. How did he know what to do? He did such a great job. How did he become so good at something he was never trained in? When I think this way I am forced to descend down the long dark stairwell of sorrow, loss, grief, sadness... But not for long. Jesus comes to my rescue. His promises bring me back to the reality of His victory. So, now I focus on LIFE, HEAVEN (I'm sure satan hates that, and I love when he's not happy and I have something to do with it.) James Drummond Burns looked at death/life this way: he said" "I've been dying for 20 years and now I'm going to live." On his deathbed D.L. Moody said this: "Earth recedes, heaven opens before me... this is no dream... it is beautiful, it is like a trance. If this is death, it is sweet. There is no valley here. God is calling me, and I must go." Isn't that cool? Then I am left to ponder the moment Levi entered into His presence. I love this part of losing a child. The part where my mind's eye sees him walking, running, playing, worshipping, being loved on by Jesus Himself. Man, I love that!!! I wonder what it will be like for the rest of us. I wonder what we'll do first.

There's a song by "Mercy Me" (a Christian group) it goes like this:

I can only imagine what it will be like when I walk by your side,

I can only imagine what my eyes will see when your face is before me.

Surrounded by your Glory what will my heart feel?

Will I dance for you Jesus or in awe of you be still

Will I stand in your presence or to my knees will I fall?

Will I sing Hallelujah, will I be able to speak at all?

I can only imagine... when all I will do is forever worship you... I can only imagine.

When I sing this song I am transported to that day when I am finally at the place I was living for, longing for, made for... Ahhh

We have been trying to decide what will be written on Levi's tombstone. It's a strange thing to think about. It's so final. It's really written in stone. What if we change our minds? What if six months down the road we think of something more fitting? But we have prayed about what the Lord wants on it... I started to think about my ring, the ring Jeff bought for me a couple of days after Levi left. It is a simple silver ring with purple stone in it. Every time I miss Levi I look at it and think of him as my "treasure in heaven, stored up, protected where nothing and no one can hurt him ever again... So that's what will be on his grave. *"Store up for yourselves treasures in heaven... for where your treasure is there your heart will be also."* (Matthew 6:20,21) Oh, what a treasure we have stored up... and our hearts are there also... LEVI LIVES will be written at the bottom so when we go to the grave site we will not be brought to sadness but to a longing for the day when we will join him in eternal victory, praise, peace and joy.

In 2 Samuel it tells about David and his sadness when his son was sick. It says, *"David pleaded with God for the child. He fasted... he spent his nights lying on the ground and would not get up... on the seventh day the child died. The servants were afraid to tell him, how can we tell him he might do something desperate."* David found out. And he got up from the ground, washed, changed his clothes and went into the house of the Lord and worshiped. He then went home and ate. His servants were shocked. They asked, *"Why are you acting this way? While the child was alive, you fasted and wept, but now that the child is dead, you get up and eat!"* I love David's response: *"While the child was still alive, I fasted and wept, I thought, 'who knows?' The Lord may be gracious to me and let the child live. But now that he is dead, why should I fast? Can I bring him back again?"* And then here's my favorite part: *"He will not return to me, but I will go to him."* YES,YES, YES!!! We will go to him and once again, we can't wait.

### February 2, 2002

It's Saturday morning. Caleb and Jonah have baseball tryouts today. It's going to be really strange to "go back" to the baseball thing. It was at the beginning of baseball season last year that we first noticed that Levi was stumbling and closing one eye. We were at Jonah's baseball practice and Levi fell about 50 times. Graci would just help him up off the ground and then they would continue playing... sometimes I wish I could go back to that day and do it all over again. I probably wouldn't change many things, I would just want to have 9 more months with him. Nine more months of knowing he was there when I open my eyes in the morning. Nine more months to take advantage of the fact that I could hug him and hold him any time I wanted to. Nine more months to stare at him all day, watching him smile, hearing him laugh, touching him over and over again...just because I could. If I could do it all over again I would...no, I can't go there it hurts too bad and I can't go back. What's done is done. Whenever I allow my mind to take me down the cruel road of "shoulda, coulda, woulda" I spend the rest of the day hating myself for the millions of mistakes I've made in the last 5 years but didn't notice because I could always "do it over," there was always tomorrow to do a better job loving my kids. But now, my "do over" time is finished with Levi. So, I have to pray that Jesus will bring to my mind the times that I did the right thing, times that I showed him I loved him. Times that I threw away the list of things to do and went to the park, sat on the swing in the backyard, went out for ice cream... man I miss him... how he used to get so excited about the smallest things. A trip to the park was as good as Disney World to him. I love that about him. I love how he loved to sing while we drove down the road, I love how he loved to kiss us all. He would hug and kiss right smack dab on the mouth every time. He would put his chubby hands on my cheeks, look right into my eyes, down deep into my soul and kiss me on the lips. There is no limit to what I would give for just one more of those kisses. Just one more...heaven and the chance to kiss him again seems so far away. So, for now, I'll focus on the family I have. The chances I have now. I am praying that my eyes will see the beauty of life rather than the dread of death. The cry of my heart is that I will not waste the time that has been given to me for Caleb, Jonah and Graci while grieving the time that is no longer mine with Levi. Lord, help me to "hug the living."

The other day Jonah and I were going through the "Levi box" and he picked up Levi's hat, put it on and started walking around the house with it on. He came to me and said, "Can this hat be mine from now on?" I was curious as to why the sudden interest in this hat so I asked, "Why?" He said, "So that when I die you can put it in your 'Jonah box' and cry for me." Oh

# Levi's Legacy

Lord, how did we get here?

You know all my life as a mother I have gone through a certain grieving process. Of course it hasn't been the death type of grieving, but what I call "grief of seasons." I look back at when my children were babies. That "season" of our life is over and I miss it. I hope I made the most of it but know that if I didn't it's too late to go back and "fix" anything I've done wrong or redo any missed opportunities to love them a little more. I'm feeling that way right now. Levi is part of one of our seasons and we must go on without him. The shock of that reality is horrible...from now on our seasons will come and go without our "little man."

I guess this whole thought process is a picture of what it will be like at the end of our lives. When we stand before the Lord we will suddenly realize that "what's done is done." Will we be ashamed or wIll we confidently stand knowing that we chose the truth and loved Him? Rita Springer sings a song that goes like this: "Lord, when my life is through I hope You will be pleased with me. Whatever came my way in all that I've been through I held on to You. The voice of my Shepherd I will follow, the hand of my friend I will take. The hem of Your garments I will kiss Lord for all of my days. In the darkest time you have been my fire that I can depend, you saved me with your love and washed me with your blood and I will obey. Here I am, so in love with serving You. My desire is to please You Lord. My desire is simply to obey"... That is my prayer knowing that when we stand before the Father we will not be judged according to how much we endured but how much we loved Him through what we endured. May my life be a "bow" before my King. Lord, help us to teach our children to see Your face in everything. May all of our "seasons" be Christ filled with as few regrets as possible. Lord, turn our "dark night" of sorrow into a depth and intimacy that we have never known. Surely, You will turn our weeping into joy (John 16:20) and our mourning into dancing. (Psalm 30:11)

Graci's prayer at lunch the other day: "Father, thank you for our food...Jesus, would you whisper in Levi's ear that we love him? Amen. Yes Lord, would you do that for us?

~jami~

p.s. Please continue to pray for Caleb, Jonah and Graci. Their loss is unbearable at times. I see it in their eyes. Sometimes we laugh and get silly together just like we used to when Levi was here but then it gets quiet all of a sudden. We stop laughing because someone is missing... no words are needed. We all just quietly feel the pain of knowing his sweet laughter is no longer with us. We miss it but can do nothing to get it back. It's so hard.

## February 6, 2002

I am looking out the window, it's cold and rainy. I look inside my heart and it too is cold and rainy. I feel sad to the bone. I miss Levi. I miss him soooo bad. It even hurts to type his name because I see his face in my mind. It's been such a long time since I've held him, seen him with my eyes, told him that I love him and "experience" his reply. It would start with his eyes, they would say "I love you too," then his mouth would say, "I love you," and then the arm…oh, that sweet chubby arm, the one working part of his body would reach up for a hug. His hugs were priceless because they cost him so much. They took more effort than everyone else's hugs. But he never denied anyone the gift of one.

Last night I went up to do my usual "check." I had already kissed and prayed for them all but I always go back upstairs for one more "look." Every mother knows what I'm talking about. The sweetest moment in the day. The time when you look at your children while they're sleeping. They're warm, they're fed, their teeth are brushed, they're bathed and now…they're resting, dreaming, peaceful.

I stood in the hallway, looking into Levi's old room. The light from the hall was shining in on the empty bed. How I long to see him sleeping. How I long to have the hope that he will be waking up in the morning and coming down with his sleepy face and baggy pajama pants, the "bed head." Oh how I miss the mornings with him… with all of us together. The dreams of them all growing in character. I have written on the wall in their room the Knight's creed, it says in big, bold, red letters: "Live pure, speak truth, right wrong and follow the king…" I wish I had the privilege of training him a little longer. Oh to have that responsibility again…

It's been almost 7 weeks that we've lived without him. It seems like 7 years… I feel like I have been searching, rummaging, scraping for purpose. I am trying to find my "place." Who am I now? A part (a very large part) of me is gone, never to be retrieved again. I feel guilty sometimes that I hurt and feel so lonely because I have 3 other children left. Why do I feel so empty? Why can't I focus? Why can't I pour myself out on Caleb, Jonah and Graci and just be glad that Levi is in heaven and taken care of? I do pour myself out on them but there is someone forever missing. I can't look past the emptiness that is there. I try but I can't imagine that it will ever be possible to love on them at the depth that I do and not be brought to the memory of my Levi. They're a "package deal." It is impossible to love one without the other coming to mind.

Oh Lord, the rain is falling outside. It is constant today like the pain in my heart. Will you flood my heart with your love? Will you rain on me your presence? Will you come to my rescue, and when you come will you bring Levi or at least the peace of knowing that he is well. You are the only One who can bring healing to this broken heart of mine. Give me the courage I need to face the day the courage to live… It takes more than I thought just to get up in the morning.

He is "shaking" what can be shaken and what remains is who I am… *"Therefore, since we are receiving a kingdom that cannot be shaken let us be thankful and so worship God acceptably with reverence and awe, for our God is a consuming fire."* Hebrews 12:28,29. Lord, let my foundation be found in You. Let it be true of me that You are at my core. You are my core. Third Day sings a song that has become my prayer: "Take my heart and make it feel, take my faith and make it real, take my eyes and help me see all the love surrounding me. Don't let me go, hold me close to where you are, don't let me go take my heart take all of me. Take my loss and take my gain, take my trials and take my pain, take my life and let it be all that you would have for me…"

# Levi's Legacy

I know that I "bleed" a lot on these updates. It is my hope that someone out there that is going through a time of darkness will find comfort in these writings. Comfort in knowing that they're not going crazy or if they are they have company in me. (ha ha ha) Maybe I can be a "pioneer" in pain. I heard a quote one time that said, "You can tell who the pioneers are because they're the ones with the arrows in their backs." Hopefully my "arrows" will draw others to the knowledge of Christ and the hope of His healing.

~jami~


## February 9, 2002

Jeff came home yesterday and was telling me about his day. He told me how he went to Levi's grave. He told me how he had taken a valentines gift to him. He had written him a note and left it there. He got in his truck and cried and cried for an hour or so. I was broken to picture in my mind him standing over the cold ground talking to our son. I asked God the same old question I always ask, "How did we get here Lord?" Is this really our story? If I remove my family from this "story" and let it be someone else's for a minute I think, "that's so sad." But then I am sobered to think that's us. That is our life. That is our little man's body in the ground. That's us leaving valentines on the grave of a 5 year old boy. Once again I ask "how did we get here Lord?" Just a year ago our story was a beautiful one. We were the family that was the envied one. We were the story of victory. We were the "dream family." And now, we're everyone's worst nightmare. I'm my own nightmare. Once again, "how did we get here?" I not only miss Levi, I miss the dream. The perfect family. I sinfully, miss the envy of others. You know what I mean? Other people used to say to me, "You're life is so perfect. You have a wonderful husband and 4 beautiful children..." I don't hear that anymore. I hear, "I'm so sorry, everything turned out this way..." If I tell someone that I don't know about what happened to us they say, "Oh, that's so sad." And you know what I say? "Yeah, it is isn't it. You know why I say that? Because it is. It is so sad. And it's my story.

The weird thing is this: When I was in the "dream life" I had this emptiness. I wanted more. I was very in touch with the incredible blessings that the Lord had smothered us in. But it was deeper intimacy with Christ that I longed for. Two weeks before Levi was diagnosed I remember praying, "Lord, I want more of you, I want to depend on you, I want more depth..." I had no idea what I was asking for. If I did I wouldn't have asked. I guess that's why the Lord doesn't let us know what He has for us. If we knew what was coming would curl up in the fetal position and never come out. Even in my sadness and wondering I feel Him "growing me up in Him." Sometimes (okay, most of the time) while all was "well" in our life I would have a really hard time longing for eternal things, "storing up treasures in heaven." What did that mean? I thought it was a really cool verse but had no idea what it really meant. I have come to know that it is absolutely impossible to "long" for eternity and heaven when we are living in our own virtual heaven here with circumstances that go with our flow. You know what I mean? My heart has always had the tendency to run wild. I picture it like a kite just rolling with the wind, who knows where it might end up, probably stuck way up in some tree. Maybe crashed in a lake but it was all a mystery which way it would go... In some way Jesus lassoed my heart. He brought me back to solid ground. He held me down and said, "Jami, Focus!!" You want depth? You want intimacy? Then, come...

I have envied the intimacy that Jesus and the Father had but have all my life settled for the "pale imitation" of Christianity. The "icing on the cake" Christianity. The "blessing without sacrifice" Christianity. Madame Guyon (a sixteenth century writer) wrote this: "When you can sit before Him while everything is falling down around you...when you can come before Him and worship Him without the distraction of self then will the test of commitment begin to be established. Then will begin the true journey of the Christian Life." It's hard to imagine that the Lord would actually allow "darkness" to come into our lives. But scripture clearly tells us of His dwelling in the darkness. 1Kings 8:12 says, *"The Lord said that He would dwell in the thick darkness."* In Exodus 20:21 it says that Moses approached *"the thick darkness where God was."* What is up with that? I thought only the devil did the darkness thing. But Alan Redpath (an English writer) says, "The devil has nothing to do with this kind of dark times. God has brought us to this experience. He wants simply to replace us with Himself." That's what He wants – to empty us of ourselves only to fill us with His fullness. Francois Fenelon (in the 1600's) wrote: "God does not transform you on a bed of light, life and grace. His transformation is done on the cross in darkness, poverty and death." At the end of Job's "nightmare" he said this, "I had only heard of you before but now my eyes have seen you." (Job 42:5)

So, I am brought to the conclusion that He is bringing us to a place of "coming out" a place of finding Him on our own rather than trusting what we hear at church on Sunday. When we go through this "dark night" we can't take someone else's word that the Lord is who He says He is. No way! You have to find it out on your own. And that's the way He wants it. I picture Him motioning His hands saying. "come on, come on, now I've got your attention, come to me, seek me out, find me on your own. Don't believe everyone else, even if they're right, I want you to KNOW me on your own." That's the "narrow gate" I think. I have heard and read about that gate but I was hoping that after we walked through the gate the path would become soft and easy. Nope, it's not that way. The path is hard, crooked and dark. But He is on it with us.

The bottom line is: *"Whoever shall seek to save his life shall lose it, and whosoever shall lose, or surrender, his life shall preserve it."* John 12:25. My "dream life" is the lost life here. I always hoped that if I were pressed to "lose" or "surrender" my life He would find me faithful. I just never thought that I would be asked to "lose" my sons life, or my "dream life." It seems like it would be easier to be a martyr unto physical death. Then I would be with Christ. But this way I am left to continue on this path that is dark, scary, and unknown to me. But the Lord says this in Isaiah 42:16 *"I will lead the blind by ways they have not known along unfamiliar paths I will guide them: I will turn the darkness into light before them and make the rough places smooth. These are the things I will do; I will not forsake them..."* Yet another verse to hang on to and trust Him through. May He find my heart faithful to Him. Every day is a choice. Every thought has to be brought captive to His ways. Lord, may I stand for You, my King, even in this...even this, my "nightmare come true."

I became my own only when I gave myself to another." C.S. Lewis

# Levi's Legacy

## February 16, 2002

The tombstone was put in yesterday. I'm confused... should I be excited? We've been trying, for 6 weeks to make all the final decisions to get it over there. Now that it's there how am I supposed to feel? It seems so final. (Probably because it is.) I'm glad there's a marker to honor Levi but it represents the verification of death. It's almost as if he didn't seem as "gone" before but now the tombstone verifies it. He's gone.

Jeff goes to the cemetery almost everyday. It makes him feel closer to Levi. Yesterday he said he had some work to do in the morning but the whole time he was working he couldn't wait to go "visit" Levi. "I just had to get there", he said. He drove into the cemetery and saw the tombstone from a distance, he parked real quick and then ran over to see...he laid down on top of Levi and cried. He said, "I just laid there remembering all the times we used to wrestle together, play together, wishing I could be with him now." He ended up laying there for an hour. Sweet, sweet Jeff. I hurt for him. I hurt when I imagine him laying on Levi's grave, crying, hurting, longing for that "one more moment." I've only been to the grave site twice. It's so hard to go. I feel a blanket of pain fall over me when I go. I can't even begin to imagine how I'll feel when I see his name on a stone with his birthday and deathday. It's a heavy thing to see your child's name with two dates next to it.

Have you ever noticed all the "roadside memorials" there are these days? I used to wonder why people put up crosses on the side of the road. I used to think it was...well... silly. But once again I am put to shame for my harsh thoughts. Now, that I am left without Levi I understand...they do it because it's all they can do. How else can you honor someone that you loved so much and are now suddenly without? They do it because it's the place where they took their last breath on earth. It has suddenly become a sacred place. You don't normally get to choose your "sacred place." but we did. Our "sacred place" for Levi is my bed. I sleep on his "memorial" every night. I am so grateful that the Lord gave that to us. Other people have to go outside in the cold and sit on the hard ground with cars zooming by to contemplate the last breath, the last thought, the last moment here on earth. But not me. I go to my nice warm, cozy room with soft pillows and Levi's favorite blanket (the one with the silky edges). He loved our bed. Sometimes we would get home from running errands and he would run inside and just get in our bed (our bedroom is on the main floor right next to the den) He would sink into all the pillows and search the covers for the "cozy blanket" and just rub the satin edges between his fingers. He would have such a satisfied look on his face. I loved it. Even his last day here he was laying on our bed and struggling for each breath but he stretched his hand straight out towards the covers. It was his sign that he wanted me to put the silky part of the blanket in between his fingers. I can't remember but I'm sure he was holding it when he took his last breath...I wonder if there are "cozy blankets" in heaven. I hope so.

In my groping to find something of Levi to hold on to I realize that I will never be satisfied with anything here on earth. (Of course, I already knew that.) What I really want I can't have right now...but there's progress in my heart: If I were given the choice I wouldn't want Levi back. If God came to me and said, "Do you want me to raise Levi from that grave to be with you?" I would say, emphatically "NO." I don't want him to come back to this sinful, fallen earth. I want to go to him (in the Lord's perfect timing) The Lord is putting in me a well thought out desire for heaven. On the days when I hurt in almost unbearable proportions and I long for Levi I think about Heaven and all its fulfillment. I remember that "better is one day in His house than thousands elsewhere." Joni Ereckson Tada says, "The art of suffering is the art of readjusting your expectations of the here and now." I am learning to expect less and less from this place. But every day I look more and more forward to Heaven. I'm not saying that I'm gonna just sit here and wait to die. NO WAY!!! My prayer is that the Lord will continuously "restore the joy of my salvation" so that I will be used to the fullest by Him to bring more and more people into His Heaven. *"May He turn our hearts to Him, to walk in all His ways and keep His commands…and may these words of mine, which I have prayed before the Lord, be near to the Lord day and night, that he may uphold the cause of His servant…so that all the people of the earth may know that the Lord is God and that there is no other."* I Kings:59-60 May our hearts be fully committed to Him until the day we are fulfilled… satisfied in Heaven. Lord, use us. Let Your Kingdom swell to overflowing with souls that came to trust you because they saw Your faithfulness, tenderness and kindness to us in the midst of our suffering.

~jami~


**February 21, 2002**

just thinking…

My updates/journals are therapy for me. But even after I have written my feelings down and I think I have "gotten it out" there is something there that I can't put my finger on, I can't express, something I missed. I'm sure there's a lot "in there" that will take years to find expression for but today I think I can see something that I have never thought of before. There's something else that I miss that I have not put on "paper…" When Levi was first diagnosed he was just a regular 4 year old (at least in how he handled the brain tumor). But as time went by he changed drastically. The sicker he became the more incredible he was. The more he suffered the more he became a "man."


**February 24, 2002**
…finishing the thoughts…

You know what's funny? The last update was accidentally sent to Mel to go on the website… We were getting ready to go out of town and I could hear Jeff upstairs walking (pacing), waiting for me to get ready. I meant to put those thoughts in my "draft box" but I guess I sent it incomplete. So, if it's okay I'll finish up the thought pattern I started:

As Levi got sicker his character started being developed in ways I never could have imagined. He became more and more self-less. He was more loving. He never complained. He cared so deeply about people. Good grief he was five years old, it would have understandable if he was preoccupied with himself. But he wasn't. What a great guy he was. I really, really, really liked him.

The Lord had given us a closeness that was beautiful...heavenly...spiritual. I would try to explain but instead I'll "read" you a letter I wrote to him in my journal Feb.19, 2002:

> Dear Levi,
>
> You're gone. You're just not here. I miss you so bad. We had practically become one in our last days together. I am left in a "severed state." Even worse than the physical separation is the emotional separation We understood each other so well, almost perfectly. I knew and translated every look on your (sweet, chubby) face, every twitch of your eye. And you knew my heart as well... you always knew when I was afraid or sad but trying to cover it with a smile. I could never fool you.
>
> I miss the "knowing." you. I miss the understanding. I miss communicating without words. I miss the one heart we shared... Now I am left with only half.
>
> I love you eternally,
> mommy

Remembering the special relationship we had is the latest unveiling of "missed things"... Things that he took with him...things that are no longer mine. Sometimes I feel really "ripped off" because in the last 2 months of Levi's life I met a new person (the person he had become) I met one of the most incredible people I'd ever known. I had met someone that I never wanted to live without. It was "the beginning of a beautiful friendship." But before I knew it it was over. Out of my grasp. Irretrievable...a tragic ending.

So, here I am again, trying to choose to keep the sorrow "at bay" so that it doesn't completely take me over. This "dark thread" of loss/suffering woven into my life is still a great mystery that I long to unravel but I can't. It's funny, this split in my personality: normally my athletic background makes me want to be strong, kick, fight, push through this part of my life. Kinda like the bumper sticker I saw on the back of a truck the other day, "If you can't dodge it, ram it!" But my mothers heart makes me just want to lie down, look at pictures, remember and cry. Which way do I go?

Stephen Olford said this: "Suffering is definitely a problem to be reckoned with. If the pain leads to resentment and resistance then the outcome is depression and despair. On the other hand if the pain leads me to prayerfulness and patience, then the result is maturity and victory." Paul asked/prayed over and over for his "thorn" to be removed. The answer from heaven was: *"My grace is sufficient for you, My strength is made perfect in weakness."* (2 Cor. 12:9) Levi's death is my "thorn." I asked/prayed for it to be removed (for Levi to live) but my answer was the same. And so now I live strictly by His grace in my weakness, trusting that His ways are the best...

*"The Lord...is righteous; He does no wrong. Morning by morning He dispenses His*

*justice, and every new day he does not fail."* Zephaniah 3:5

*"There is an appointed time for everything. And there is a time for every event under heaven... he has made everything appropriate in its time."* Ecclesiastes 3:1,11

I am still praying that I would "feel" His presence more and more. It is another weakness of mine (the need to feel, that is). Oh Lord, it is my prayer that you would "capture me" again." That my heart would open wide again and I would be completely "seized by the power of Your great affection" for me.

~jami~

**March 1, 2002**

I haven't written in a while because the last couple of days I've been struggling and didn't want to "talk." I have been hammering God with questions that I don't have answers for. He has seemed stoney silent and I've been MAD at Him. I mean, what's so difficult about a little communication, a little "presence?" I have been feeling like He doesn't love me because He doesn't seem to be "talking" to me these days.

Yesterday was Caleb's birthday, tonight we're having a spend the night party and tomorrow we're taking the kids to a skate park. I want Levi with us. I don't want to celebrate another year without him. But I can't have him and that is making me angry I guess. I feel frustrated that time is just going on. Pretty soon I'll need to let go (whatever that means) and continue life but I don't want to, I don't know how to. I feel like a traitor to Levi when things seem normal. This time next year maybe I won't cry everyday. But I want to. If he was worth loving he's worth grieving over for the rest of my life.

I have a picture on my dresser. It is a picture of Levi in ICU at the hospital. He has a ventilator in his mouth and an NG tube in his nose and various other tubes running in and out of his body. He's asleep and I am laying next to him, kissing him, holding him. It's my favorite picture because I'm doing in that picture what I would give all I own to do just one more time. I try to think about the fact that I will kiss him again in Heaven but I'm very "now" minded these days. I'm like a spoiled child. "I know I'll hold him again in Heaven, but what about now, what do I do about my feeling of empty arms?"

I was sitting on the couch in our den, reading, thinking, writing... I was at a loss for words to describe where I am in my relationship with the Lord. Graci went into the bathroom. I didn't think much of it. Then, I heard her hitting the toilet paper roll. She does that all the time when there's no more toilet paper. There she is sitting on the toilet, finished with her "business" and then she notices that there's no paper. Most would yell out "hey, if anyone is out there could you get me some paper?" or maybe even just get up and go get some herself. But no, she just keeps hitting the card board roll. I guess she thinks if she hits it enough then paper will just sprout forth...I know that's a weird story to tell but that's where I am in my relationship with HIM. I just keep "hitting the roll" hoping that my needs will be met, that out of the blue His presence will overwhelm me and I will feel again and the pain and emptiness will be more bearable. But no…nothing…

I have another mental picture that I have painted that helps express where I am. It's the age old potter and the clay analogy. Of course, He is the Potter and I am the clay. I was a vase. I was on the wheel, spinning. I had shape from the trials in my life. I wasn't perfect, I wasn't beautiful but I had character. I was growing and changing…but then out of the blue he got that string that potters use to cut clay and He just leveled me. He just cut me off the wheel so low there's nothing left but the wheel and a little clay residue. So, here I am trying to get my bearings on what just happened…?????

I am so confused right now. Just when I think I should be healing I run into a wall of sadness and notice my incredible lack of understanding. What is God doing? What is He thinking? Does anyone really "know" Him? Will we ever understand any part of Him? "I am bedraggled, beat-up and burnt-out. I am an inconsistent, unsteady disciple whose 'cheese is falling off her cracker'. I am bent and bruised, feeling like my life is a grave disappointment to God." (Brennan Manning)

I read a verse that really encouraged me today: This is what the Lord says; *"Let not the wise man boast of his wisdom or the strong man boast of his strength or the rich man boast of his riches, but let him who boasts boast about this: that he UNDERSTANDS and KNOWS me…"* Jeremiah 9:23-24 There is hope!!! To me, this insinuates that we can know and understand Him to some extent. I don't need to "know and understand" all. Just something, anything… Madame Jeanne Guyon said, "If knowing answers to life's questions is absolutely necessary to you, then forget the journey, You will never make it, for this is a journey of unknowables—of unanswered questions, enigmas, incomprehensibles. And most of all, things unfair." I agree partially but not completely. If we just sit back and say "it's just that way" we miss the "wrestling match." It is true that we might not have all the answers but isn't it also true that we "find" more of Him in the desperate search for answers?

A Scottish preacher was preaching a sermon after the sudden loss of his wife. He admitted that he did not understand this life of ours. But still less could he understand how people facing loss could abandon faith. "Abandon it for what!" he said. "You people in the sunshine may believe the faith, but we in the shadow MUST believe it. We have nothing else." I've never met this preacher but I "know" him. Just like I "know" Job. Just like I "know" every other shadow dweller. We are the desperate souls trapped in the desert hoping for rain. But you know the cool thing that I've noticed about the desperate? They get the good stuff if they wait long enough. Like Job. He was described as a "perfect man." Perfect!! He communed with God. But it wasn't until after He had gone through "the desert", "the nightmare","the dark night of the soul" that he saw God anew. Remember what he said? He said: *"My ears had heard of you but now my eyes have seen you."* (Job 42:5). I'm still waiting for the time when my eyes will "see" Him.

I know this is just a lot of rambling thoughts but the lack of organization represents the state of my heart. Some days all I know is that I miss Levi. Other days all I know is that I miss the way things used to be between me and my Heavenly Father. Today, it's both. I long to feel God love me and I long to let Levi feel I love him...

~jami~

## March 5, 2002

It was 20 degrees while I was sitting on Levi's grave. As I suspected it was incredibly eerie to see his name on a slab of granite. It seemed so inappropriate for his name to be among all those dead people. I never knew them, I never loved them, trusted them, honored them. But there they were right next to one of the most loved trusted and honored people in my life. They have no idea how blessed they are to be "associated" with even the shell of such an incredible little man...

I didn't stay there long because it was so cold and as I was sitting there it became more and more painfully obvious that he was not there. Of course, I already knew that but I guess I was hoping that something really special would happen while I was there. Like, I would see an angel that would say, *"Why do you look for the living among the dead?"* or maybe the Lord would give me some really cool encounter with His Spirit. I know I sound like I've lost my mind and maybe I have but remember I'm desperate so the sky is the limit to what I hope for.

When I drove away I felt like a negligent mom, leaving him there. How does your heart know that you are no longer responsible to take care of your child? It can't. It goes on longing to cuddle, hold, keep warm...love, take care of. Five years ago Levi was born on November 13. Also born on that day was this "mothers heart" for him. I feel like there should be a tombstone right next to his. It would read, "Here lies the heart of a mother, the rest of her still walks, breathes and lives but her heart died on the 20th day of December along with Levi"...

It's been over two months and I thought it might be a little easier by now. I'm not sure why I thought that but I was hoping I could at least look at his pictures without the feeling of a burning knife going through my heart. The knife is still there and hotter than ever. I look at pictures and it's so weird, the face that was so incredibly familiar is no longer something I see everyday. The chubby cheeks that I cleaned every day, the teeth that I brushed, the eyes that were there to meet me and look into my soul every morning, that little nose that had begun to look way too small for his newly large face... I saw it every day. It was "what I did." It had become "my day"... His face looking at me waiting patiently for his bath water to be run and his carrot juice to be juiced. It was all so "everyday" and now it's never. It's all a far away dream. I miss the "everyday-ness" of him, the expectancy of seeing him, knowing that he is right in the next room, right next to me on the couch or bed. I changed his broviac dressing every three days. Man, would I love to have that responsibility again. I go over it in my mind. I remember every detail of the process. I remember how he loved it. His eyes would close and he would say, "That feels so good, mommy." He would ask me several times a day when it would be time to change his dressing again. I'd say "We just changed it today." He would roll his eyes back in disappointment that it was so far away until the next "change." Then, he'd say, "I just love how it feels, it tickles"... Sweet little man didn't know that most kids hated having their dressing changed...

Pictures used to be sweet little reminders of how beautiful my children are. Now they are the most precious things I own. If the house were burning down I'd (we'd) grab the kids, my bible, the pictures and then my journals. The rest I could do without.

*"We are under great pressure, far beyond our ability to endure, so that we despair even of life. Indeed, in our hearts we feel the sentence of death. But this happened that we might not rely on ourselves but on God, who raises the dead."* (2 Corinthians 1:8,9). Lord, help me to rely on you. I have prayed that HE would be the air that I breathe. I didn't consider the fact that if He became my "air" I'd have to get used to breathing HIM instead of the air I was used to...

~jami~

### March 7, 2002

I remember watching "Gone With The Wind" when I was a little girl. I always loved that movie/book. I remember being taken aback by life on the plantation. So many people constantly having parties, barbeques, gatherings... It was a beautiful place full of color, life, love, beauty, ease and blessing... I don't think there was a time that Scarlett (in her self absorption) took a minute to look out across the vast plantation and recognize the blessing of it... It wasn't until after the war, death and destruction that she stood up on the hill and looked out across the land to see what was left of the dream she had once lived. Now, it was gone, gone with the wind...

That's the way I feel. I look out across the desolation of my life. I close my eyes and see the "plantation" before. A beautiful and complete picture of blessing. But I open my eyes and scour my new truth, what is left. The "trees" in the field are still burning from the fire. The beautiful garden is no more. The house is falling apart from the attack. The beautiful dresses are now made out of old drapes instead of the finest store bought fabrics...there is death... It is such a sad and empty time. But it is now that Scarlett (me) has to grow up. She can no longer depend on others to serve her. She has to do it herself. She has to "pull herself up by the bootstraps." But I have one up on ole Scarlett, I know that I can't do it. The desolation is too great. I have to go further and depend on the hand of God Almighty. I am too weak to help myself and my family.

I'm not surprised by the disaster. I expected it. I knew that if we loved God and were committed to Him "come what may" we would be attacked. Elisabeth Elliot's husband, Jim was murdered while taking the gospel to the Auca Indians. She said this: "Every man and woman who chooses to trust and obey God will find his faith attacked and his life invaded by the power of evil. There is no more escape for us than there was for the Son of God. The way Jesus walked is the way we must walk. Again and again we will find ourselves looking to heaven in bewilderment and asking the old question "WHY?

*"In this world you WILL have trouble. But take heart! I have overcome the world."* John 16:33

I still don't understand why the trouble comes. If I were God I would make the believers, the lovers of God have no trouble. But I guess if there were no trouble we wouldn't realize our deep need for Him... I don't know... I have so little knowledge, so little understanding of HIM. Evelyn Underhill said: "If God were small enough to be understood, He would not be big enough to be worshiped."

All this rambling to say: My life is desolate, I don't understand, I am sad and afraid... but I will worship Him.

~jami~

**March 15, 2002**

It's been almost 3 months since Levi left us. The cemetery and the "happenings" there have become very familiar to us. In the last three months there have been about 5 new people buried close to Levi. It seems like there are so many children. It's heartbreaking. I feel this urge to leave notes on the tombstones of the others and ask them to call me. I feel like I know them in a way because we share such an intimate place of brokenness.

I drove by the cemetery yesterday on my way to pick up the boys from school. There was a funeral going on right next to where Levi is buried. I wanted to go in and see who they were. I wanted to know their story. I wanted to hug someone. I called Jeff to tell him that there was "someone new" being buried close to Levi. He said, "I know, it's a baby." I was shocked that he knew. He had been there the day before and seen the new hole being dug. " It was a little tiny hole", he said. Man, that hurt. Just imagining the pain, the shock. The "not rightness" of it. Baby caskets shouldn't be... but they are and that really bothers me.

I planted new flowers in the yard yesterday. The pansies I pulled out were the same pansies that Levi and I planted together in the Fall. I remember, I laid a blanket out in the grass for him to lay on. We talked, laughed and planted. I loved that day. I loved having him there in it. I remember as we went inside after working in the yard all day. I was carrying him in the door and time froze as I looked at the Maple tree in our front yard. The leaves were bright and beautiful, I loved the sight of it. But I knew the seasons were changing and soon the winds would come and blow those beautiful leaves far, far away. In my mind it had a much deeper meaning than horticulturally speaking. I guess my heart had snuck down to the thought (before it had to) of what the coming seasons would bring... And so it has come to pass. The tree is bare. The grass is yellow. The leaves on the ground are brown. My heart is broken, barren, blowing back and forth with the wind. Levi is gone...

...But Spring is coming. The leaves will soon be green along with the grass. The geraniums will be bright red and the begonias pink. (Levi's favorite color was pink, it made me nervous that he liked pink instead of blue.) :) For him Spring has sprung. Surely Heaven is filled with all kinds of pink flowers and little boys can love them without people questioning their masculinity...

# Levi's Legacy

Graci and I took a walk around the neighborhood yesterday. We walked up to the pool where we have so many sweet memories of all the kids playing together. We sat on a big rock right outside the fence. We weren't talking we were just looking at the pool. I was wondering if she was thinking what I was thinking. Right then she said, "I miss Levi." It was confirmed. We were thinking the same thing...

As I imagined life without Levi that day I looked at the Maple tree and the promise of changing seasons it seemed unfathomable. How could we live without him. I still feel that way but I am learning to trust the Father with the unfathomable things in my life.

I'm learning, growing, changing...I know the Lord is using this pain in my heart to work out His plan. When the tragedy first began I would liken myself to the man who was driving a truck up a mountain. The winding roads dropped off 500 ft. The man was a nervous wreck. He was trying to keep his truck on the road but it became too much for him and he lost control. His truck slipped off the road and fell 500 ft and exploded into huge flames. The driver was thrown out of the truck and was holding onto a tree branch. As his body was dangling above the burning truck he called out to the road above him, "Is anybody up there?" The voice of God Himself said "Yes, I am here. I will help you but first you must trust me and let go of the branch." The man was silent in thought for a while. Then, he looked up toward the road again and said, "Is anybody else up there?" – That was me. That's still me in some ways... I could go on and on about all the things I've learned but the main thing is trust. I don't trust Him because I want to. I trust Him because I have to. I am at a humble place. It's the "where else do I go place?" Once again Job and I are together in this... *"then Job fell to the ground in worship and said, 'naked I came from my mothers womb and naked I will depart.' The Lord gave and the Lord has taken away; May the name of the Lord be praised."* Job 1:20-21

~jami~


## March 23, 2002

Today is the one year anniversary. One year ago today we went to Jonah's baseball practice, I remember watching Levi play with Graci, he would fall and Graci would help him up, then a few minutes later the same thing... he fell about 20 times in an hour. By the time practice was over he was completely avoiding using his left arm. Later that night when Jeff was praying with the kids upstairs I was walking into my bedroom and fell to the ground crying. I couldn't stop. It was that dry heave cry. The whole time I was sobbing I was thinking, "why am I crying, I don't know for sure anything is wrong so I've got to get a grip." After about 10 minutes I dried my eyes. Jan (our faithful Dr.) called. I told her what was happening... she said get to the hospital a.s.a.p... that was the beginning of the end.

"Time flies." That saying has new depth to it now. I've never had to say it with so much loss in the middle of the time that has flown by. As I look back at the beginning of our battle I see myself as fragile. I was fearful of so many things (one of which was one of my children dying). I am different now. Don't get me wrong. I still have fears but I have learned how to look them straight on and fight. Or maybe I should say I've learned who to stand behind...

I remember the first week of "diagnosis." Everyone kept saying "the Lord will make you stronger through this." I thought, "well, He'd better hurry up before I have a nervous breakdown." Now, I look back at my journal from "the beginning" and I see where my strength came from. It is clear that once again desperation for God was the key to survival. I held tightly to several verses but this one sums up where I was: *"I cry out to God Most High, to God who fulfills His purpose for me."* Ps 57:2 He is fulfilling His purpose for me and my family. I just never knew how hard it would be. We are all being changed through this pain... I know God is "good for" His promises. I just feel caught between the ways things were and the "promise." I figure I feel a lot like the Israelites did when they were in the desert wondering what had just happened. One day they were all excited about their new freedom and the next they were stuck in the desert. There's a song by Sarah Groves called "Painting Pictures of Egypt." The words are descriptive of how I (and the Israelites) feel. It goes like this: " I don't want to leave here and I don't want to stay, it feels like pinching either way... the place I was wasn't perfect but I had found a way to live. It wasn't milk and honey but then neither is this..."I'm caught between the promise and the things I know. I've been painting pictures of Egypt and leaving out what it lacks. The future seems so hard and I want to go back. But the places that used to fit me could never hold what I've learned. Those roads were closed off to me while my back was turned." Does that make sense? In other words: I know that His plan is perfect. I know that His promises are good (best). I know that who I was before this tragedy was not even a shadow of the person that He has intended for me to become. But I'm having a really hard time looking ahead. I'm having a hard time seeing that this "way" is good. I think I could "get it" if it weren't for the pain, the memories, the deep, deep, deep love I have for Levi. I think I could see the whole picture if I didn't long for something, anything to be the same as it was before. I even miss my other children. They're different now. Don't get me wrong. They are incredibly wonderful but they have been forced to "wise up" quickly. There is an innocence that was lost. There is a sadness hidden deep within their souls that I know is there. I want to "make it all better" for everyone but I can't. I am completely out of control. I am getting to some strange "phase" of grief where I miss Levi for everyone else. I see my sister (Lori) and how she misses the sweet bond they had, how she cries and wants "just one more chance" to hold him and look into his eyes. I miss him for her. I see my mom and dad's look of incompleteness when we go over for a visit and there's one less grandchild to come through the door. One less hug. One less kiss... I miss him for them. Jeff and Levi used to "wrestle" every night when he came home from work. I miss him for Jeff. Caleb and Jonah used to run in the house and hug Levi every day when they came home from school. They scratched his back at night. They fed him when he really got sick. I miss him for them. Graci had the privilege of being his buddy and playmate everyday. Now there's only me and in comparison I'm boring. I miss him for her. I even see other children that used to play with Levi at the ballpark. They just look at me. I know they're wondering where he is. They don't ask, they just keep looking at me... nothing is said...I just cry behind my sunglasses wishing they could play together like they did last season. I miss him for them. I saw a friend the other day that I hadn't seen since last Summer. She came up to me and said, "Where's my baby?" I thought she was talking about Graci so I pointed toward Graci and said, "there she is." My friend said, "No, where's Levi?" I had to tell her he was dead. She buried her face in her hands and cried. We hugged and cried together at the baseball field. I missed him for her. I miss him for me. I miss him so bad.

Lord,

Surely this pain will serve as the refiners fire… surely You are purifying our hearts…surely you are bottling each tear that falls, even each tear that has yet to fall you know of. You are able to keep us from falling and to make us presentable before your glorious presence without fault and with great joy. (Jude 1:24)

~jami~

**March 30, 2002**

It's Saturday morning. Everyone is still asleep. It's thundering and lightning outside. But the Lord is here with me. It's really cool, for so long now it seems like it's been sunny and beautiful outside but the storm was always raging inside of me… today it has changed, maybe for just a moment but I will enjoy his presence as I am able to feel. Today for some sweet reason of His, I FEEL. Today, the storm is outside and the quiet peace is inside.

I have had a reoccurring dream ever since Levi died. In this dream I am at Levi's tombstone. I am crying over his death. But then I do something strange. I stand and dance in worship before the Lord. I know that's strange but I do, as if to say I will worship you, I will praise you, I will trust that You are good, even in the death of my son… In my heart I have not yet been to a place that I could do such a thing. I have known in my head that He is good at all times but to dance before Him in my heart, to celebrate Him in this nightmare of mine… NO! I couldn't. I would start (in the dream) to dance but then tighten my arms to my side and stiffly walk away. But today, I feel HIM. Today my heart misses Levi terribly but I dance in my heart before the Lord. I know that tomorrow is coming and I could be in the slumps of grieving but for today. I dance. Today, I feel… It's amazing how great it is to feel when you haven't for so long.

There's a song by Natalie Grant, It is the expression of my heart: Oh Holy one, Father of the earth. Create in me a pure heart so I can come in spirit and in truth to worship you, that's what I long to do. I love to praise I love to lift your holy name from the rising of the sun and the going down of the same. Your name is great. I will bless you all my days because I love to praise. Oh Righteous one, lover of my soul , age to age forever still the same the sweetest light the sweetest melody, praising you is where I long to be. You are Holy and my lips will always sing your praise… You are worthy…

The other day Graci and I were out working in the yard. Levi, Graci and I used to do that together while Caleb and Jonah were at school. But this time it was just Graci and me. It was obvious to both of us that "someone" was missing. So, to break the silence I said, "I miss

Levi, how 'bout you?" She was looking at the ground and never looked up she just said, "Yeah, I miss him so bad but Jesus 'gots' him, no fair." How sweet is that? We sat down for a while and just talked. We talked about how great it will be when Jesus "gots" us all and we'll never have to be separated again. I love how free she is to talk about him. I love how The Lord brings healing to my heart through my other children. I see the power of God in the daily things. I see that even the smallest flicker of light will cut through the darkest night. That light is HIM. His beauty is ancient and yet so new. I am like someone who was in a tragic accident and has been paralyzed for months, without feeling in his arms and legs. But today, he can feel his toes and he screams to the nurse, "I feel something, I feel something!!!" I just wanted to share it with you.

*"The Lord will fulfill His purpose for me; Your love, O Lord, endures forever – do not abandon the works of Your hands."* Psalms 137:8

This is totally off the subject but I just heard the news that we (the U.S.) have agreed with the UN security counsel resolution to call for the removal of Israeli troops from Palestine. In other words we have turned our backs on Israel. That is really BIG and really BAD. Zechariah 12:3 says. *"On that day, when all the nations of the earth are gathered against her, I will make Jerusalem an immovable rock for all the nations. All who try to move it will injure themselves."* In Zechariah 12:9 it says, *"On that day I will set out to destroy all the nations that attack Jerusalem."* I have talked to some people who are not interested in what goes on in the middle east. They feel like "it's not our business." I have to say: It is our business. Everything that is happening in Israel is our business. It's all been prophesied so if I may just send a little warning to all Christians: Choose this day whom you will serve, the Lord God (of Israel and every true believer) or this country (the USA). Make no mistake about it, if we turn our hearts hard toward Israel we have turned our hearts cold to God Himself. If this seem a bit radical and a bit out of line then just read the Bible and you'll see… but remember: *"Blessed are all who take refuge in Him."* Psalm 2:12

~jami~

## April 9, 2002

I haven't written in a while. I kinda hated to write a follow up to the last update. It was such a "high" and I haven't been enjoying that same high on a daily basis. So, I've just kept the "not so wonderful" stuff to myself. I must admit that I've fallen into this "gotta 'look' good" mode. I've had a few people make "suggestions" on how I should do things a little differently to be more upbeat, focusing on the rest of the family or being not so sad. But since I am sad that would be a bit difficult. I've not written because I have been feeling like I can't be honest anymore. Like I've got to fake that everything is back to normal and we're all as happy as can be, we're not sad, we don't miss Levi and we're moving on to a new ministry of "be 'happy' because God is good."

But I can't! I have bad/sad days. I do still struggle with anger. I miss Levi and sometimes think my heart will explode if I don't see him soon. The Lord is working in my heart about forgiveness and compassion. I admit that HE has had to teach me countless lessons on these two issues of the heart. And I do NOT like it. I've seen that my heart is prideful and prone to turn hard and immobile. I cling to my defense and anger feeling that I "deserve" them rather than forgiving. When people make suggestions on what I "should" do to grieve more efficiently I feel like my time is up! Like I'm hurting too long and I need to forget Levi and just focus on Caleb, Jonah and Graci. Sounds really easy! But not so. I don't think the Lord would make me passionately in love with my children and then require me to cut out the Levi portion of my heart. What would that say to my other children? "If you die I'll miss you for 3 months but then I'll be over you."

I guess I need to make it clear that this website is my grieving table. I come here to sort through my heart and the pain that resides there. When I get up from this desk I do my very best to hold my head up and create a joyful atmosphere for my other children. But at the same time I don't want to teach them to be "fakers," or what I call "heart liars." How torturous it would be to require that we all "act" like God has finished His healing process and we're "done" when we are all hurting beyond words? Maybe the "be happy" theology is helpful to some (which I really doubt) but not for me, not for us. We are a changed family. We will never return to the way we were. Our hearts are anchored to heaven. Our love of this world has been weaned from us. We (I) cannot act like sadness and missing Levi is not a very real part of our daily lives.

Let me share with you one day "without Levi." – I wake up and stare at the ceiling. I still think, "Is it true? I really won't have the privilege of taking care of Levi today... ever? I drag myself out of bed and get things moving toward getting the boys to school. I open the kitchen cabinet and see Levi's favorite "cup" mingled in with the other glasses. I get the boys vitamins out and see all of Levi's medicine still there (I wish I could give it to him one more time). I make carrot apple juice and my mind takes me back to my old schedule when I would make it for him every morning...I walk past his picture 1000 times, I smile at it every time. Graci plays by herself and says, "I miss Levi" several times a day. We talk, we remember together, we cry... I walk into my bedroom and see Levi's special tray that he used to eat on. The cruel irony that there is now a plant on that tray, a plant that was given at his death. I give Graci a bath and remember how they played together in the tub every morning. I look into the closet and see his never opened Christmas presents. I turn on cartoons for Graci, it's "Bob the Builder", Levi's favorite. We read books, the same ones I used to read to Levi while we were in the waiting room at the doctors office. I look outside and see Levi's bike in the driveway. My heart leaps and then I realize that one of the other kids must have gotten it out. I get in the car and put Graci in her carseat (missing the chance to put Levi in his carseat) I go to the grocery store and calculate meals for 5, not 6. Yesterday I bought donuts at the bakery. I could only find 3 alike so I was looking everywhere for 4 with sprinkles...then I painfully realized I only needed 3. I would have searched all day if only I could need 4 again. We see a mother with 4 small children with her. I covet the completeness she has... We come home and I cook dinner. I get out the plates...one for Jeff, one for Caleb, Jonah, Le... no, I don't need one for him anymore...I hate that!!! It's time for bed. The night time routine begins...Graci first. We pray, I scratch her back and sing. She wants "nothing but the blood of Jesus" (Levi's favorite) I sing and cry. I lay in the moonlit room remembering...remembering when I would sing to both of them, scratch both backs at the same time. I tickle Graci's face. I remember how I used to do that for both of them. I play with Graci's hair, I remember how I used to play with Levi's hair...I miss his hair... I go to Jonah next, then Caleb...I go downstairs all the while feeling like I'm missing someone... I am...

Jeff and I sit and talk. Sometimes we cry together, sometimes we just remember, sometimes we just go to sleep just holding each other thinking the same thing. Words aren't necessary. We understand each other's silence. As I fade off to sleep... I thank God for my other children, more grateful than I ever could have been before, but I miss Levi and that's the fact.

All that to say: It's really hard to take someone's advice or suggestion for change. We're just living here. We can't go beyond the "call of duty" right now. We just get through each day by the skin of our teeth. We seek the Lord's healing in each painful memory, praying that the sting will fade. I have come before the Lord and asked Him to "let me go" – to release me from this intensely painful part of grieving. The Lord has not released me. He is still working out some stuff in my heart. I cannot go ahead of HIM. I just wait for my release. HIS timing is perfect. I am not! Not even close.

In summation: I am dealing with anger. I get angry when people say: "I'll tell you what I'd do..." when they've never walked this dark valley. I am surprised at the ugliness of my heart. I am ashamed at the way I seem to nurture my anger. I am shocked at the way I justify my sinfulness. It is clear that the Lord is doing some pretty major purification in my heart. But this is it!! This is one of my "chances to die" a chance to die to myself and my "rights." Lord, please don't let me reason away and excuse myself when I need to let you "pin me to the wall" on the state of my heart. My flesh wants to shout out the injustice of life and "loose talkers." I want to say LOUDLY, "Who do you think you are, telling me how to grieve?" Lord, you know my personality, you know that being quiet and gentle is not natural to me. You know me. Teach me Your gentleness. Teach me Your kindness, teach me to see from Your side of the sky. How do I focus on You and Your ways and not my offenders?

Now, I know that some people are reading this thinking, "wow, what a mess!" This is true, but I say along with Paul: *"Christ Jesus came into the world to save sinners – of whom I am the worst. But for that very reason was shown mercy so that in me, the worst of sinners, Christ Jesus might display His unlimited patience as an example for those who would believe on Him..."* (1 Timothy 1:15,16)

"I would rather be cheated (offended) a million times than develop a heart of stone." —Tim Stafford. Lord, help my heart...

~jami~

**April 16, 2002**

This morning I'm thinking of Heaven. I wonder... what will be the best thing about it? Of course, I have no idea. I can't even imagine since scripture tells us that "no eye has seen, no ear has heard, no mind has even conceived it... but if I were to think of what could be my favorite part of heaven (aside from seeing Jesus and Levi) I would have to say it would be the "foreverness" of it. Seems so obvious I know but I'll tell you what I mean: When Levi was diagnosed it's like this big huge clock started and I was trying to stop it. It was such a "hurry up and wait" feeling. I felt in a rush to be still...trying desperately to stop the chaos of life and try to enjoy every moment, stopping to smell the roses all the while the deafening silence of the "clock." No matter what I did the inevitable came to pass. Now, I look at my other children wanting to stop the "ticking." I can't help but see every moment as a possible "last." "Anything could happen," "who knows what tomorrow could bring." It's as if I want to stay ahead of any more possible pain. I have been on a mission to live a life without regret, not even one. But that is quite impossible because I'm starting to see that my greatest regret now is that I have been putting such pressure on myself to not have regrets... I've been trying so hard to make every moment useful and impacting... I knew I was not trusting the Lord to work things for His good when: I was laying on Caleb's bed with him. I was just staring at him while we were talking. I was etching his face into my mind. I guess Caleb noticed so he stopped talking and said, "that face, I love that face." It was cool that he noticed that my face was a reflection of the love in my heart for him. But then, I said, "Oh, Caleb, will you always love the Lord, no matter what comes? Will you love Him and His ways till your last day? He put his sweet hands on my cheeks and got this pained look on his face as he said, "Oh Mama, please don't worry so much!" Oh no, he saw it. He saw my lack of faith. He saw that I was not relaxed in the knowledge of God's sovereignty. He saw that I hadn't gone to the Lord in prayer and trusted that HE loves my children even more than I do...

Intimacy with God. What does that really mean? How does it bubble over into every aspect of my life? How do I get that? Ronnie Floyd says: "To know intimacy with the Father is to answer God's ancient question, even as it was put to Adam" 'Where are you?' If we are honest we, too, must respond, 'I was hiding.' In our candor, we take the first step toward wholeness as we address our true condition. We are hiding from love, hiding from pain, hiding from our desperate fear of being known, and hiding from the God who loves us – who wants to clutch us to His bosom, never let us go, the One who wants to whisper a Father's word of comfort into our waiting ears. Intimacy."

Man is that true! I hide myself in the busyness of "making the most." That seems like a good thing but like so many other things it brings me to a place of leaving HIM out. A place of seeking purpose outside of HIM. It can't be done, it always leads to emptiness. Why do I do that when I know where my hope lies? Lord, since I must hide (and it seems that we all find a hiding place somewhere) then help me to hide in you. *"Rescue me from my enemies* (of which I, myself am the worst), *O Lord, for I hide myself in You."* Psalm 143:9

I guess my "plea" for the day is: Lord, surely this path in suffering is the road that leads to deeper intimacy with You. The kind of intimacy that looks into the face of death and says, "I will not cower, my mouth will speak in praise of the Lord." Oh Lord, touch me, be the light that I live by, be the breath that I breathe, be the dream that sets me free. Let my children see that You and I have a good thing going on, a romance that is pure and confident. Let it be true of me that You are the music in my soul that cannot be squelched. Let my life be a dance that my children are drawn to. Oh that they would see very little of me and so much of You... Lord, be the courage and hope to which I boast. Teach me to live and finish well even though the longing for the day you call us home is so strong...

~jami~

### April 22, 2002

This morning I was changing the sheets on my bed. I saw the stain on the mattress where Levi had wet the bed over and over. Oh how I would love to change the sheets because he wet them... my mind carried me back to the hospital when, for days, he hadn't gone to the bathroom. The nurses gave him 2 enemas and oral laxatives and still, nothing. I remember waiting for him to go "poop". I remember praying about it. I remember when he finally went. Wow, what a mess! Head to toe, top of the bed to the bottom, a HUGE mess. I remember the nurse (not our usual nurse) seeing it and saying "eew gross!" Clearly she had never known the sweet gift of the "proof of life." To me, that mess meant he was ALIVE! yeah poop! He's ALIVE! I enjoyed that mess like you wouldn't believe. If only I could have to do that again... I would, I would Lord, If only I could do it again. I miss being his nurse. I miss the honor and privilege of "doing" for him. I miss his sweet voice. I miss him saying, "mom, you're the best mom ever," and putting that chubby arm up for a hug. I miss him! I miss him! I miss him!

I have a picture of him at the pool with swimmies and goggles on. I look at his body and how familiar it is to me. I can remember every square inch of his body. I look at his belly button... how sweet and cute it is. I never knew to stare at it. To see it move up and down with each breath. His little square feet, "Fred Flinstone" feet. His always chubby hands that seemed to be screwed into his arm. They were always too big for the rest of his body. I love those hands. I wonder if he would have lost his teeth by now. You know he couldn't wait to loose those teeth so he could be just like his big brothers... how strange it will be when Graci loses her teeth when Levi never did.

My heart hurts so bad today. So sad. I hate how life just keeps going on. Sometimes I chart in my mind how far we've made it without him. I'm surprised at how we have survived and want to reward myself by "waking up" from the nightmare. But the truth is still hard and strong, going on is all there is. It's like running a race that will never end. No matter how tired I become I can't stop. I have to keep going further and further away from when he was alive. The trouble with life is that it just keeps happening whether I'm ready or not. I have no choice but to *"hold unswervingly to the hope* [I] *profess, for He who promised is faithful."* (Hebrews 10:23)

Obviously, today is a sad day for me. It's windy but beautiful outside, the perfect day for a kite and a trip to the park. That's something that would really throw Levi into a tizzy of excitement. I can hear him in my mind. Once again he would say, "mom, you're the best mom ever." We bought a really cool kite for the kids the day before Levi was diagnosed. We've never flown it. I think I'll get it out and make a memory with Caleb, Jonah and Graci. Maybe we'll tie a note on it that says, LEVI, WE MISS YOU AND LOVE YOU SOOOO MUCH!! And then we'll fly it as high as we can into the "heavens." If only it were that easy. If only we could get a "note" back saying, I LOVE YOU TOO, I MISS YOU BUT WE'LL BE TOGETHER AGAIN SOON, VERY SOON. LOVE, (YOUR VERY COMPLETE) LITTLE MAN, LEVI. Wouldn't that be cool?

I will "Endure hardship as discipline; God is treating me as a son/daughter... God disciplines us for our good, that we may share in His holiness. No discipline seems pleasant at the time, but painful. Later on, however, it produces a harvest of righteousness and peace for those who have been trained by it." (Hebrews 12:7, 10,11)

I have a special friend (Jamie Hahn) who lost her daughter (Christy) to cancer about 6 years ago. She has been gracious and loving to share her heart and loss with me. She still misses Christy, she still hurts but she seeks the Lord, she loves Him and she trusts Him. Whenever she writes me, she signs her letters "fumbling victoriously." I love that. It says soooo much in just two words. I feel that way today. I'm fumbling TERRIBLY. But because of my hope in Christ it's victoriously. :)

[Yes I am] Fumbling victoriously,

~jami~


**April 28, 2002**

This is the first Spring we've had without Levi. Sometimes I actually forget that he's gone. I think of him and I feel joy at the mere thought. The "flower" that is joy in my heart goes from a bulb to a plant, then a bloom and then the flower withers and dies when my heart and mind come together and remember the truth, he's not here. Sometimes I just say, "Caleb, Jonah, Levi and Graci." I love to hear myself say their names together again. It's so incomplete to go through the names with one missing. Sometimes I write their names all together like I used to. We got our new neighborhood directory this year and it didn't have Levi's name in it. I hated that, it doesn't seem right. It's not right!!!

Jonah had a bad day yesterday. I noticed he was quiet all day. He kept to himself and was irritated with everyone. Later, he and I laid down together on my bed and talked. I found out that he just "really misses" Levi. He said, "Do you know what one of the sweetest things that I miss about Levi is?" I said, "what?" "Those cheeks, I loved those chubby cheeks of his." We laid there and talked about all the other things we loved about him. It was good for Jonah, it was good for me.>>>>> Caleb and Jonah were talking about whether or not they will play basketball this coming Winter. Jonah said, "Is it okay if I don't play?" I said, "you don't have to play any sport you don't want to play and there's plenty of time to make that decision..."

Caleb chimed in, "besides, we might not even be alive then." I was shocked at his thought so I asked him, "why do you say that?" He explained, "well if Jesus comes back we'll be in Heaven with Levi anyway." (Sounds good to me!!!) The other day Graci was showing me how good she could snap her fingers. She actually put her fingers IN my ear to show me how loud it was. :) I remembered her and Levi practicing snapping their fingers and competing on who could be the loudest. So, I asked, did Levi know you could snap so well? She immediately looked up toward "heaven" with her hand fully outstretched and snapped. Then, she yelled, "Did you hear that Levi?" Sweeeeeeet! Today, Caleb said (out of the blue), "Do you know which was my favorite Thanksgiving?" I said, "which one?" His response was healing to me. He said, "Levi's" (meaning the one in the hospital, ICU)

Graci was singing in bed this morning, I was listening without her knowing it. These were the words…"Levi loves me so much, he wants to hug and kiss me because he misses me, I want to hug him and kiss him too but we can't because he is there and I am here…"

When we go to the cemetery to water the flowers that are in front of Levi's tombstone Graci walks around looking at the other tombstones. Then when it's time to leave she says, "Waaaaiiit!" and runs over to Levi's tombstone and kisses his picture (on the front of the tombstone) and says "bye Levi, I love you," and then runs to get in the car.

We were all talking the other day and Caleb said, "I wish we could start all over again." I wish it could be the day they first told us that Levi had a brain tumor. It would be hard to do it over again but at least we would have him for nine months longer. At least he would be with us now."

Sometimes when I meet new people that don't know about Levi I think to myself, "If only we had met 4 or 5 months ago, then they would have met the 'whole' me, not just part of me."<<<<>>>> When Jeff sees 5 year old boys out while he's working he can't stop staring at them, wondering what Levi would be like now. "Would he be inquisitive like that little boy?" "Would he ask lots of questions?" or "would he be shy and not talk at all?" What would he be like if all this had never happened?

These are all just fleeting moments, thoughts or comments that I wanted to capture and never forget. They are our hearts spoken. They are our "way" to keep him alive and here with us. May it never end… may we never be" healed" so much that we don't talk about him, remember him, long for him, sit still and picture the way we were when we were all together.

~jami~

**May 3, 2002**

It's Friday. It has been a really bad day today. Not circumstantially, I just miss Levi. I have started to notice a pattern: I go about 4 days without letting myself "go there" (I'm afraid of it, I guess… I pull back from the pain… I hate it) but then I'll have a day like today. I've had a lump in my throat all day. On the verge of falling apart with the longing to see him. I keep really busy but then in the end there's no running, no hiding, it catches me and I have to give in and "go there." I have to cry from my soul, I have to. I can't choose not to, my body won't let me. I'm a prisoner to raw grief. So, here I am at my grieving table hoping that I can find expression for how I feel today. How deeply I hurt. How endless this pain is. Will my heart ever find relief this side of heaven? Will the sting of my loss ever be satisfied? Oh Lord, I miss him so bad, What do I do with that Lord, what do I do with that?

It was this time last year that we were making plans to go to Disney world. I remember getting out the calendar, deciding which week would be best. The squares that represented days were so empty. What would the future hold? I never knew the future before but all of a sudden I noticed it. I felt so useless to save Levi's days. I remember thinking: When will it be Lord? When will we have to live without him here with us? What will be the day that I will never forget? (ironic that it turned out to be my birthday) I would only let myself think that way for a little while and then I would run back to the safety of the hope of his healing. I still had that option. "Man, those were the good ol' days"... I knew a day was coming when that pleasure would no longer be mine. And here we are. I have a new found respect for drug addicts that have to go "cold turkey." I've never had a physical addiction but my addiction for my children is surely comparable. I need to have them with me. All of them. I need Levi back. I feel like I can't breathe without him. Like a drug addict "without" I would lie, cheat, steal and kill to get him. But of course, none of that would bring him back. I am behind bars. I just have to go through it. I might not have the shakes and a cold sweat but I do feel that same "panicky", desperate, "gotta have him or I'll die" feeling... I need a "Levi fix" but it's not for sale... I HAVE TO wait...

I got an e-mail from a friend of mine. Her little girl has a brain tumor also. All their efforts for medical treatment have been exhausted. These are her words: "Dear Jami, ...I think about you almost constantly and as I watch my little girl slowly dying my heart breaks for you too because I know you still hear your little Levi's voice and see his smile. There are times when I do not know where to get strength or how to pray"...

My heart is seared. I don't read her words, I feel them. Sweet precious lady thinks of me in her pain. I am speechless. After all I've been through you would think I would have some really great words of wisdom. But no, nothing. I have NOTHING... I know that my words and my wisdom are powerless in the face of death. I've learned that less of me and my words is best.

*"Oh God, you are our God for ever and ever; You will be our guide even to the end."* (Psalm 48:14)

It's funny, I've spent most of my Christian life preparing myself to be willing to die for Christ, to be faithful no matter what. But I've learned that dying would be (seemingly) easy. It's living that has turned out to be the hard part. I know that sounds really depressing, but it's not, really. I'm just learning what it means to join Him in His suffering. Learning being the operative word, not learned. Lord, teach me truth in the inner parts; teach me wisdom in the inmost place… let me hear joy and gladness; let the bones you have crushed rejoice… (Psalm 51:6 & 8)

Please pray for my friends, Steve, Veronika and Julia (9 years old / brain tumor).

Still fumbling, still victoriously,

~jami~


**May 12, 2002**

Well, it's here. Mothers day! Sweet precious day of honor. This is a day that Jeff and the kids usually can't wait for. Jeff usually takes them all out a couple of days before to search for a special gift from each one of them and then one from him. I remember years ago, before Levi and Graci were born, Jeff and I found ourselves in one of the biggest arguments [fights :)] we've ever had. He had forgotten Mothers day! Sin of all sins… I remember sitting him down and saying "Look, you can forget my birthday, you can forget our anniversary, you can forget Christmas. But please, please, please never forget Mothers day. It's who I am, it's what I do. It defines me and all my dreams." Jeff of course was a puddle of "I am so sorries" He said , "I didn't know, I just didn't know it was so incredibly important to you." My response was, "I didn't either, but for some reason it is now."

That was the beginning of Mothers Day becoming almost as big as Christmas at our house. I remember last year! Oh man what a special day! They ALL (Oh how I wish for all) went out and did their annual shopping. The each had their own special gift to give: candles, flowers, slippers, pretty smelling soap. But then they brought in the table and chairs that I had been wanting for our back deck. If you could have seen their faces. They were so proud of this fine purchase. That was it! That look of excitement on their faces was the greatest gift of all. There is no price tag large enough for the beauty of their excited faces…

Today, I feel so sad. I know there will be one less face, the chubby one with the crossed eye. Oh how I loved that sweet face, the heart behind it. Last year I wondered if I would be blessed with another year with us all together. I had no idea what it would mean to come to this day without him. I had no way of knowing that this amount of pain, sorrow and emptiness would be mine… that it would bombard our special days as well as our "every days." C.S. Lewis, in his book A Grief Observed wrote: "I have forgotten the reason, there is spread over everything a vague sense of wrongness of something amiss. Like in those dreams where nothing terrible occurs – nothing that would sound even remarkable if you told it at breakfast-time – but the atmosphere, the taste, of the whole thing is deadly. So with this, I see the berries reddening and don't know why they of all things should be depressing." In other words, there is a cloud over him, he and I share it. It is a cloud of grief that goes everywhere with you, uninvited even. It can only be understood by those who have grieved and now try (without success) to resume life as it was. I wonder if I'll ever have the power to remove the cloud when absolutely necessary. Like today. I am still the mother to three other sweethearts that are loved no less that the "little man." How do I remove this ever-present cloud? What a stage this is for me. The Lord is stripping me. I am becoming more and more bare before Him. Just when I think "that's enough" He strips me down a little more. Surely He does this by His hand of mercy. Taking away the old, the ugly, the dead parts of my "tree" so that someday, I will grow beautiful fruit. But for now I feel ugly, torn down. I find comfort in what Elisabeth Elliot said in her book "A Path Through Suffering," ...Every stage of the Heavenly growth in us is lovely to Him; He is the God of the daisies and the lambs and the merry child heart!"

Lamentations 3:31-33 says *"For men are not cast off by the Lord forever. Though He brings grief, He will show compassion, so great is his unfailing love. For he does not willingly bring affliction or grief to the children of men."*

"The Lord is merciful to us in our grief. He always proves Himself worthy of the trust He calls us to have in Him." (Zig Ziglar)

I have learned in the "day in and day out" of my oh so deep loss and grief, that relentless darkness that surrounds without mercy, That deceiving sense of abandonment by HIM. Yes, I have learned that He is actually calling me to a deeper place in Him. He's waiting to see if I'll reach out to Him, without inspiration and warm fuzzy feelings toward Him. I have found that His heart is for a people who are constantly running after Him. And the truth is we won't run after Him unless we're trapped, scared, lonely... desperate. Once again desperation has served me well. It speaks an ugly truth about me and everyone else I guess. We are only faithful to Him because He puts us in desperate situations. "On the whole, God's love for us is a much safer subject to think about than our love for Him. Nobody can always have devout feelings... But the great thing to remember is that, though our feelings come and go, His love for us does not." (good ol' C.S. Lewis)

> Dear Father, I long for Levi, I long for all of us to be together again. I long for it here because I don't know how to long for it there (in Heaven). It seems so far away... Help me please. Help me to live a holy life, to finish well. To finish strong. To finish desperate for You. Oh that on that day You would find us faithful. Oh Lord, would you make us ready, a pure and spotless "bride" for You our "bridegroom." Surely these ugly scars and hurts on my heart will be beautiful to you. Surely you will use them to make me clean before You...*"fine linen, bright and clean"*...(Revelation 19:7) We've come a long way Lord, but we've got a long way to go... Keep me.

> In Jesus' name and by His blood.

~jami~

Blessings and sweet joy to all you Mothers. "Swim" in the blessings that they are. I know I will...

P.S. Jeff, Caleb, Jonah and Graci all came down the stairs to my "quiet place" one at a time. First, Jonah with 2 dozen red sweetheart roses, then Caleb with 2 dozen yellow sweetheart roses then Graci with carnations with baby's breath. Then came Jeff, sweet Jeff with his precious "love offering"…a big red rose to represent Caleb, a big red rose to represent Jonah and a big red rose to represent Graci. Then, with a shaky voice and tears he said: "The big pink rose is from Levi, you know how he loved pink"…


**May 20, 2002**

Graci came into my room holding a picture of Levi to her chest. She took one last look at his sweet face before she looked up at me and said, "I don't want him to be in heaven any more, I want him back here with me." That little peek into the heart of Graci spoke mounds to my heart. It expressed how I have been feeling for days. I think I'm "hitting the wall." Everything seems to be "getting back to normal" as far as everyone around me. Everybody seems okay with Levi being gone. Everyone seems to have "fallen" for the pat answers… "he's in a better place"…,"All things work for good"…, "This too shall pass"… all these are true, wonderfully true but oh so hard to walk through. They're words, (true) words that make Levi no less gone…

Levi had a Winnie the Pooh watch that he loved but he just could not keep up with that thing. Every two or three weeks "out of the blue" he would say, (in his squeaky little voice) "Hey, where's my Winnie the Pooh watch?" So we would look for it but to no avail. Then, about 2 weeks later it would show up somewhere. It would be like Christmas for him! "Hey, I found it! Here's my Pooh watch." He would push the button on it that would play the Winnie the Pooh song and we'd "enjoy" it for a while until he misplaced it again and we'd go through all that again 2 or 3 weeks later… well guess what I found while cleaning house this week? But Levi wasn't here to get excited about it. Graci and I played the song and remembered our "little man." The words to the song say, "silly old Pooh all stuffed with fluff"… I used to sing that to him when he had gotten so chubby that he looked all "stuffed with fluff." Maybe that's why he loved Pooh, he could relate to him…

…it's not getting any easier. My heart is still crushed, the hole is still there, maybe more than ever…it's getting harder, I think. You know why? Because Levi being gone is "common" now (to everyone else, that is). But missing him is such a big part of my day. "How happy I would be if I could forget to remember how sad I am." Emily Dickinson.

Another strange thing is happening to me… I am loving Levi more. I didn't think it was possible but I do. I think of all his special traits. I remember his voice. I remember how he hugged so tightly, I remember how, every time I would leave the house without him he would say, "But I will miss you so bad"… I remember how he loved us so completely and without reservation. I admired him. He is a hero to me, because he made me slow down and enjoy the small pleasures of life. He brought out so many good things in me… there's a part of me that is forever tucked away because it was the "me" that only he could bring out. I miss that part of me… it was good.

Obviously, today has been a very sad and teary day for me. At dinner my sweet Jonah prayed…"Dear Father, Would you bless our meal and would you tell Levi we love him and we miss him...and Lord, would you tell my mom that he misses her too? Amen" Then he looked up at me and said he misses you mom, he loves you so much...

Graci is starting to want to go to the cemetery more often. As she was getting ready for bed tonight she said, "tomorrow I want to go see Levi in the 'casket.'" (she thinks we can go to the funeral home and see him in the casket like at the wake when we really miss him bad and can't "take it" anymore.)

Caleb still keeps pretty quiet about Levi but he is starting to enjoy the memories. We all laugh together when we remember his squeaky little voice. We all try to imitate him and that brings laughter along with a sweet reverence and honor for the "little man."

I've found that there are only a handful of people who can "handle" talking about Levi. The rest avoid the subject. I understand it's hard for some people but it makes him seem "more gone" when the subject is avoided. I have great respect for the ones who are courageous enough to "enter in" with me..."*It is better to go to a house of mourning than to go to a house of feasting, for death is the destiny of every man and the living should take this to heart.*" Ecclesiastes 7:2

I am learning to "take His yoke" and learn from Him. I am so weary and burdened...I know He will give my soul rest because He truly is gentle and humble in heart." I just don't understand why He does what He does... I will continue to trust Him...

~jami~

## June 6, 2002

It's Thursday morning. Last night was a very hard night for me. I just missed Levi so bad. We were on vacation last week and then this week has been the "recovery week." I've kept myself so busy... I knew it wouldn't be long before I would "break down." Last night I went out to water the flowers, it was quiet, nothing but the crickets. The stars were beautiful and there was a soft breeze. The beauty of the night made me slow down, come to a screeching halt, actually. All of a sudden, all of the pain and sorrow that I have "put off" for the last week and a half hit me right between the eyes. I felt so sad I could hardly bare it. I went to the sidewalk in front of our house and wept (weeping is so much stronger than just crying). I cry everyday still but this was one of those out of control, soul cries... I looked up at the stars through my tears and felt sooo angry at God. My thoughts were, "You made the stars, you made the crickets to sing in unison, you put the whole earth on its axis and worked its "schedule" to have day and night, winter and summer... You created the human body with all its intricacies... You could have healed Levi in the blink of an eye. But you chose not to and that makes me so mad at You. My heart is broken, my understanding of you is lacking... Do you care that I am in constant anguish? Do you love me? Why can't I have Levi? Why can't we be a whole family again? How will I ever recover from this depth of heartbreak?

I have a sign in our den that says "It's A Wonderful Life" then under it there are pictures of our family... It was such a "wonderful life" and I miss it so terribly. I look at the pictures of Jeff, Caleb, Jonah and Graci and they seem to have such dimension because I can take my eyes off the picture and then look at the "real thing." But Levi's pictures seem so flat and with NO dimension because that's all I get. There is no looking down from the wall to see a living breathing version of the picture. I miss the "real" Levi. I miss him so bad. It's been so long since I've seen him move...

Jonah was looking at the pictures in the den and called me into the room and said, "Mom, which picture do you like the most, the one with Levi and Graci eating a green popsicle or the one of Levi and Graci hugging? I said, "I think I like the one of Levi and Graci hugging because you can see their faces better." He said, "I think I like the one with them eating the popsicles because I know how much he loved green popsicles so I know he was happy." Then he looked at me and said, "If I could just hug him one more time..." We sat down and hugged each other for a while, no more words...

Last night was bad, really bad. But the verse that came to me this morning was: *"Let the morning bring me word of your unfailing love, for I have put my trust in you. Show me the way I should go, for to you I lift up my soul."* Psalm 143:8

I know this update is pretty sad and depressing, but it's true. There's one thing I can say about our (the Lord and my) relationship since Levi left; "It's real." Which is good, I'd rather be honestly ugly than a beautiful liar. I feel like the velveteen rabbit, "I may be ugly but I'm real." And there's a freedom in that. My hunger for intimacy with the Father is stronger than ever. Even in my anger, frustration and lack of understanding He calls me. He calls me to pursue Him in this uninvited shadowland of my life. And so I do, fearfully, timidly and still with so many questions as to why it had to be this way. Like the Shulamite woman (Song of Solomon 3:2) *"I will get up now and go about the city, through its streets and squares; I will search for the one my heart loves."*

Still fumbling,

~jami~


**June 11, 2002**

I know that my last update was quite the "downer." Since then, I've had friends write me and encourage me, countless people praying for me, just loving on me and I am so grateful for such love, such commitment. What a blessing to have friends and family that love us at such a level. Friends who choose to "walk" with us through this. It must be kinda depressing to read about such intense sadness. Some stand at the door of our grief and say "Nope, no further, it's too sad and I don't want to feel sad..." (and that is completely understandable.) But, then there are those of you who walk through that door with us, taking your hearts to a place that it has not yet been called to go. I've learned so much from you because if I were to search my heart before Levi was diagnosed (and if I was honest) I'm not sure I could have chosen to go into the darkness of someone else's heartbreak. I hope I would, I hope I could,

# Levi's Legacy

I hope I would have been just like y'all. It's funny, courage and strength have taken on a new "face" for me now. I see it in your tears, I read it in your letters and e-mails, I hear it in your prayers for us. If Levi had not had a tumor and then gone, I would have never known this side of love. I would have never seen the "profile" of Christ's face. Thank you, thank you, thank you... I pray for you, showers of mercy and grace from the Lord...

This morning I was reading in 1 Samuel 1. I was reading about Hannah and how she cried out to the Lord for a son. She wept in a way that the priest, Eli thought she was drunk (I can relate to that, Jeff says that when I weep for Levi I sound drunk). Before she had a son she said to the Lord: "..."if you give me a son, I will give him to You for all the days of his life..." My first thoughts are, "You'd better watch what you say, girl, don't bargain with God. Do you know what it means to give your son over to the Lord? It's a permanent thing..." But of course, that's because I'm a coward these days... The Lord gave Hannah a son (Samuel). Then, Hannah said: "I prayed for this child, and the Lord has granted me what I asked of him. So now I give him to the Lord. For his whole life he will be given over to the Lord." I've read this passage many times in my life but it takes on new meaning now. It hurts more, It's deeper and more intensely admirable that she kept her word.

When Levi was 6 weeks old we dedicated him to the Lord. We turned him over to be used for the Kingdom of God. The Lord took me at my word but I'm having a hard time keeping mine. I'm back pedaling big time... Oh Lord, give me the strength and courage to be half the woman that Hannah was. Help me to lift my eyes toward You and "boast in my condition." The condition of emptiness. The painful condition of "being on Your anvil." When Levi was first diagnosed I wrote on my chalkboard, "There is no circumstance that God has not allowed in order to shape me more into the image of Christ. I will use it and use it well because He loves me enough to change me." That was so much easier to say and do when I still had Levi to hold. This is where the "rubber meets the road" and I am praying that the Lord gives me what I need to carry on. I pray that I will say along with Hannah, *"My heart rejoices in the Lord; in the Lord my horn is lifted high... There is no one holy like the Lord; there is no one besides You; there is no Rock like our God."* (1 Samuel 2:1-2)

I long to be transformed, "redone" into the person that HE has called me to be. I want the Lord to use me to the fullest in this. I long to be released from this cage of grief so that I can finish His plan for my life. I want so much to be a "bondservant to His freedom" but today I am only a pathetic lump of self-pity, missing what used to be instead of longing for what is to come. Not to be too dramatic but, my soul groans too deeply for words to be released from this bed of sadness and grief. Charles Spurgeon said, "Groanings which cannot be uttered are often prayers which cannot be refused." I like that, it gives me hope.

...just another thought about where I am in missing Levi... I've tried and tried to figure out this emptiness inside me. I haven't been able to put it to words... hopefully this makes sense to you – Home... home is not the town we live in, it's not the street we live on, it's not even the house we live in. It's our family. It's being together. So, if home is togetherness then we're living out of a suitcase in a hotel, wishing we could go home but it's been foreclosed, sold, lost... it's not ours anymore...I wonder if anyone else who has lost a child feels that way too?

It is true of me that I am a "clumsy griever" but I am setting my face like flint before Him. I will not turn around for another. I will only learn to live in heavier pursuit of my true home, living worthy of the home being prepared for me, where Levi is waiting, where we will be together again...

~jami~

## June 24, 2002

...just thinking about surrender and all that it means, all that it used to mean before Levi had to leave and all that it means now... I remember years ago singing along with the song "I surrender all" thinking it was such a cool song. It was so much easier to "surrender all" back then because the Lord had not asked me to give my son, I had not yet tasted the bitterness of sickness and death. Surrender was a warm and fuzzy word that meant I give up a few bad habits and He blesses me beyond words. I thought there were boundaries on this surrender thing. It's all different now. Surrender is such a scary word to me now. What will He ask me to lay on the altar next? What if I can't conjure up the courage to open my hands to Him? What if I turn out to be a coward and fail to finish well? I know He will give the strength as I need it but sometimes the hope that I depend on so deeply doesn't seem like enough to get me through the day. I want a physical touch, I want a chubby little man's hand to hold, I want Levi, I want him underfoot today... the hope of tomorrow is sometimes (most of the time) too far away... surrender... it's such a big word now. Lord, I know that what You do is right for me but it feels so wrong. It feels so empty. I have been reduced to a beggar... a beggar at Your table of grace. There is just enough to get me through the moment. If You gave too much I would stand and walk away, become prideful that I am a survivor. In my desperate hunger I know better. I stay close to your table, close to your feet. Being a beggar is not as bad as I thought it would be. Maybe it's because You are a kind master...

I am so looking forward to Heaven... I am looking forward to it for myself, for our family but especially for the children in our family (Caleb, Jonah, Graci, and my sister's children, Carli, Casey and Sydney)... yesterday they got into the "Levi box." They were looking at his little clothes. I watched without them knowing. Their eyes were wide as they remembered. They smelled his clothes as if hoping for a smell to take their minds back to when his smell in the house was common. Jonah was looking at a picture of Levi... my heart broke to see him rub his finger across Levi's face in the picture wishing it was still an option to touch his real face...

We (7 of us) were driving down the road when out of the back seat Sydney (only two days older than Levi) said, "When I die and go to heaven I will tell Levi how much y'all miss him..." Sweet, sweet, tender Syd. She's at such a loss without him... so am I.

I still catch myself "painting pictures of Egypt." I think of life before the diagnosis. I think of life as he became sicker and sicker. I remember in the "last days" when he was frustrated because he couldn't express himself, his paralyzed body, the constant pain of watching him hurt. It was very difficult to say the least but I would take it all back today if only I could. It's selfish I know, I just long to communicate my love and devotion to him. Even if he couldn't talk to me I just want to be able to tell him what a privilege it was to be his mom... then I think of him and how much he needed to be relieved of that sick body. I think of all the things the Lord spared us from, no seizures, no chemo, no radiation, relatively no pain for him... the blessings of him seeing angels, seeing him lift his little chubby hands to praise the Lord (I have no greater joy than to see that my children are walking in the truth. 3 John 4). But then my rebuttal to myself and God is but why did he have to get a brain tumor in the first place? Then I remember the miracle we saw... the man we met in Levi... the depth we have grown... I wouldn't trade the nine months of watching Levi go from a boy to man. I wouldn't trade what the Lord did in our own hearts. What a predicament that is, isn't it? I can't live without him but I can't give up what the Father taught us through his sickness and death.

I know this is a confusing update, jumping from one thing to the next but I guess that's where I am, still confused, jumping from praise and gratefulness to regret and sorrow. I am certain of one thing though, I have never longed to know HIM more than I do right now... I find comfort in 2 Corinthians 5:1-5

*"Now we know that if the earthly tent we live in is destroyed, we have a building from God, an eternal house in heaven, not built by human hands. Meanwhile we groan longing to be clothed with our heavenly dwelling... so that what is mortal may be swallowed up by life. Now it is God who has made us for this very purpose and has given us the Spirit as a deposit guaranteeing what is to come."*

~jami~

## June 30, 2002

random thoughts...

My brother and sister-in-law (Dicky and Betsy) just had a baby boy! Luke Barlow. I'm so excited for them. (I'm excited for me) I'm excited that they are experiencing the wonder of new life. I remember when all of my children were born. Everything was new. The lack of sleep was difficult but what a great reason to not sleep. I remember when Graci was a baby, it was doubly exciting since she was a girl. All three boys were soooo excited about having a girl in the house. Every morning they would run into our bedroom to see if it was still true "we really do have a baby girl in the house." "Oh Mommy, I can't believe we have pink stuff in our house." "Yeah, and maybe someday we'll have a 'barbie' in the house too." Every morning was like Christmas in our house, I loved it... I loved the feeling I had when I woke up and realized it was true, the dream was true. I do have three incredible little boys and now a beautiful baby girl... ahh

That was a season of life that will never be forgotten. But, like all seasons it ended and life got a little more difficult every day. Having four children under the age of 6 had it's difficulties to say the least. I remember trying so hard to "enjoy" that time in my life. I would talk to older, wiser women and they would tell me to relax and enjoy these days because they would pass so quickly and be gone forever. They might as well have been speaking another language because I couldn't imagine these days and their never ending list of things to do being over. And enjoying these days??? ha, that was way out of the question. Everyday became exhausting and hard to get through. Some days I would cry out to God and say, "Lord, I can't do this, it's too hard and too constant, how do other women do this and come out with any trace of sanity? How will I make it?"

But those days eased up. We moved into a bigger house where I could homeschool. The kids were 8, 6, 4 and 2. We were just coming into a new season of life, things were getting easier because Caleb and Jonah could help now, they were so becoming so grown up now. Levi's personality was just starting to blossom and Graci was the exclamation point at the end of our "sentence." I was just starting to really enjoy and appreciate each one of my children in new way…

…*There is an appointed time for everything. And there is a time for every event under heaven, a time to give birth and a time to die… a time to weep, and a time to laugh… a time to mourn, and a time to dance… He has made everything appropriate in its time.* Ecclesiastes 3:1-11

I sure loved when the mornings were wonderful and everything under the sun was new. I loved waking up and being pleasantly surprised that the dream I thought I was dreaming was my reality, everyday. Now, I wake up in the morning and have to come to "grips" with the fact that the nightmare I was having is my new reality… everything is new again but it is hard, unpleasant and dark rather than refreshing, exciting and "pink."

Don't get me wrong. I hope I don't sound like a whiner and like I'm not excited about our new little "baby Luke." Not at all. I guess that's kinda my point… There is a newness, a hopefulness that came to my heart when he was born. I guess what I'm trying to say is that the Lord has given me a greater appreciation for life and birth that I couldn't have had without experiencing sickness and death first. The miracle is bigger and brighter now. The gift of a new little one is so much more precious. Now I know what those older wiser women were talking about when they said, "enjoy these days…" I think I just became older and a (little) wiser. Who'd a thunk it?

~jami~

**July 19, 2002**

It's been quite a while since I've written. My lack of writing is not because I haven't wanted to or certainly not because I haven't had anything to say. It's just that busyness has been the medicine of choice lately. If I keep moving the pain can't catch me. Of course that only lasts so long before I wear out and the truth is always there waiting. Then I am forced to face the brokenness of my heart and the fact that some things break and can be fixed but then other

# Levi's Legacy

things (like my heart) will never be fixed. It will forever be damaged...

I was remembering some of the sweet things Levi said and did while he blessed this earth with his life. I remember the day a friend of mine came over for a visit. Levi didn't really know her. But for some reason he just "took to her" right away. He sat in her lap and just stared at her. He talked to her the whole time she was here, he was "smitten," I guess you'd say. Then, he looked at her and said, "Remember when I didn't know you?" She replied, "Yes, I do." Then, sweet little man said, "That was soooo sad." He was only four years old but he knew the sadness of being without someone you love. He had only known her an hour or so but he knew that he liked her and life without knowing her must have been really sad.

I'm having this weird low point right now. I have been speaking at various bible studies and luncheons... I love it. I love to share where I am in this journey. I love to hear other peoples stories. But I've started to notice that after a speaking engagement I am exhausted and very, very sad for a few days. I think it's because I rummage through the pain and talk about it, cry about it. It's like therapy for me but when it's over I still have to go home to no Levi...

There's an old quote that says: "Life is like a wild horse either you ride it or it rides you." Sometimes I don't know if I'm riding or being ridden. I guess it's at those "feeling ridden" times that I turn my heart toward HIM out of desperation and say: "It's too much Lord, I feel overtaken by life and all its pains, the quickness of it all, the injustice of it. What if one day I get up in the morning there's not enough courage to get out of bed again?" Sometimes my heart gets lost in the shuffle, the whirlwind. I feel sorry for myself... but then I remember Nahum 1:3, *"...His way is in the whirlwind and the storm..."* so my "arrow prayer" is: "Lord, hold me close, I can't see where I am, I can't see where I'm going, I'm spinning out of (my) control... let me be in yours...

Ignatius said: "My dear Jesus, My Savior is so deeply written in my heart, that I feel confident, that if my heart were to be cut open and chopped to pieces, the name of Jesus would be found written on every piece"... Let it be true of me Lord...

I still can't see or feel my way in this journey but I am clinging to Him, I will not turn around for another, I will set my face like flint before Him. He will answer the cry of my hunger for Him. S. J. Hill says, "He will never bypass the one who refuses to be denied the deeper things of His heart."

In "Enjoying God" (S. J. Hill) He tells of a woman who was meditating on the image of the apostle John leaning on Jesus' breast (John 13:25). She said to the Lord, "It just doesn't seem fair that John was the only disciple who got to lean on Your chest and hear Your holy heartbeat." She felt the Lord respond by saying, "John was the only one who wanted to." I like that because the Lord has put me in a position of "want." I want to hear His holy heartbeat, I want to love what He loves, I want to hate what He hates. I want to fulfill what He wants to fulfill in my life. I have no idea what all that means but I think I'm at least headed in the right direction...

fumbling, fumbling, fumbling,

~jami~

# Levi's Legacy

**July 22, 2002**

Conversations with a three year old…

Last night Caleb and Jonah spent the night with their "Mama" and "PaPa," Jeff went to the driving range to hit some golf balls and Graci and I just "hung out" together. At first we were going to play golf together but we couldn't find a golf ball. So, we played golf with a baseball (we have plenty of those). Then, we "bagged" the golf clubs and just started to toss the ball a little. Graci has a great little arm so I said, "let's get the gloves out." I started to teach her how to throw properly…"Graci, step with your left foot and throw with your right arm"… before long I was rolling, laughing at her "form." She could not seem to step and throw at the same time. She and I were donkey laughing, then all of a sudden she looked at me and said, "You know Jesus and Levi are watching us…" So, I said, "Really? what do you think they are thinking?" Her response was, "Well, I think they're playing together and laughing at us…" Ahhh what a sweet thought…

After the baseball thing turned out to be a bust we decided to lay down a blanket and look up at the sky. The sun was going down and the sky was turning pink, purple, and blue. It was beautiful. The colors and clouds were changing so quickly that we would close our eyes and count to ten and when we opened our eyes again the colors had already changed… finally we opened our eyes and the "pink" was all the way up the hill and we could hardly see it so we got up and ran up the (street) to see if we could "catch" it. We did. When we got to the top of the hill it was there. Graci said, "We caught it, now lets go home, it's getting dark." So, we walked back down the hill and sat across the street from our house and just looked at it. We just sat there and remembered what that house was like when Levi was there. We were "going over" memories. Then out of the blue Graci put her little hands on my face, pushed my hair back, looked me in the eye and said, "I'm sorry Mom." – "I'm sorry Levi's not here anymore." Sweet little angel of mine… sweet little gift of God that I so desperately love…

It's been more than 7 months since Levi left and Graci has changed drastically. I was thinking, If Levi were to come back right now, I think he would really like her and the person that she has become because of his "leaving." I know I do.

Oh how grateful I am for her. How grateful I am for my family… for so long now, I've been "deaf to anything but the shriek of my own heartache." But I'm starting to hear and see other things. I'm starting to have a grateful heart rather than a "slighted heart." There is still so much for my ailing heart to learn but for now gratefulness is the "lesson for the day." Being grateful for my "unanswered prayers" for Levi to live is hard. But surely it is right! Henry Nouwen wrote this about the spiritual work of gratitude:

"To be grateful for the good things that happen in our lives is easy, but to be grateful for all of our lives – the good as well as the bad, the moments of joy as well as the moments of sorrow, the successes as well as the failures, the rewards as well as the rejections – that requires hard spiritual work. Still, we are only grateful people when we can say thank you to all that has brought us to the present moment. As long as we keep dividing our lives… we cannot claim the fullness of our beings as a gift of God to be grateful for. Let's not be afraid to look at everything that has brought us to where we are now and trust that we will soon see in it the guiding hand of a loving God."

# Levi's Legacy

...and Job said, *"If we take happiness from God's hand, must we not take sorrow too?"* (Job 1:10) Why was that verse so much easier to read when we had Levi here with us? Why wasn't I more grateful for our complete family when I had it? Why am I profoundly sad when I see a bicycle sitting in the yard with no "little one" in sight? Why does a bright red ball sitting motionless in the street break my heart so deeply? Why didn't I notice this sadness before? Because I hadn't learned what it meant to be grateful, yet. It has taken these things to arouse my selfish heart to sit up and take notice... there is sooooo much to be grateful for. Loss has taught me this and surely the hand of my loving Father is at the bottom of this incredible lesson...

I say along with Brennan Manning: "Father, Thank you for the four seasons, for each glorious day of sunshine, and most of all for the gift of the Unsetting Son, Jesus Christ, who by His death and resurrection has set us on the road to glory."

Fumbling victoriously,

~jami~


## August 8, 2002

I can't believe that Summer is almost over. We went to Caleb and Jonah's orientation for school and I walked by the kindergarten class that would be Levi's. What a stab of pain went through my heart as I looked at all the children in their little desks, wide eyed at their new, grown up status. "Little man" couldn't wait until school. He would walk past that same classroom and say, "that'll be my room when I'm a big boy." I wanted to walk in that classroom and tell them all how sorry I was that they were missing a treasure and they didn't even know it. I wanted to tell the teacher that I was sorry that she would never get the chance to meet her very favorite student... that if she had known him for even one minute she would be overwhelmed at the magnitude of her loss... surely that class would be better if they only knew him for a little while... I know that I am better because I knew him for a little while...

Sometimes I am "used to" having three children here. But then other times I am slapped in the face with the shock of missing one. Every night I go up to check on them one last time before I go to sleep. They're usually in their own beds and I go from room to room kissing, staring, praying... but this night they had all congregated in Caleb's room (Levi's old room) they were all crowded in the double bed... 1,2,3...all of a sudden the lack of one hit me. I gasped out loud at the pain of it. I just kept saying in my heart, "there should be 4, but there's only 3." In my mind I pictured him there right in the middle just like they used to "line up" when they all laid in bed together. I pictured him with his arms over his head and his mouth opened, his chest going up and down with heavy breath, even with an occasional snore. So peaceful, they all were, unscathed by the harsh realities of the pain and tragedy life gives. It seems like just last night when I had the privilege of seeing them all together, when I would look at their little shoes and clothes laying on the floor, knowing they would ALL be worn again. But now all of Levi's clothes are in a box, never to be "warm" again. I hate that!! I hate that!! I hate that!!!

Obviously, I'm not feeling to great today. The courage thing is not enticing to me today. I'd rather curl up in a ball and cry for what used to be mine, have pity on myself for what might have been but will never be ,now… I feel sad for my other children that they have to be familiar with such loss. Just for now…when I get up from this computer I will choose to be grateful for what I have today.

Yesterday we were driving down the road… out of the blue Caleb asked if I dressed Levi before he went into the casket. At first I couldn't remember exactly what transpired in those blurry days…then I told him that "no, the 'funeral guy' did it." He was shocked and said, "Why? you're his mom, you should have done it." All of a sudden I felt angry that I wasn't allowed to. Then I felt shame that I didn't demand to be the one to dress him for the last time. Why didn't I? What was I thinking? Then my anger turned into sadness… All of a sudden I remembered the day before he died. I was getting ready to leave the house. My mom was staying with him. Every time I walked past him he would put out his arms for a hug and his eyes would well up in tears. I would say, " Oh Levi, I'll be right back…" Then he said, "but what if I don't get to say good-bye?" I had forgotten about that comment until now. Did he know that he was going soon? Why would he say that? My mind is desperately trying to remember more… then Jonah says, "I wish Levi could have died on my birthday, then your birthday wouldn't be the worst day of your life." I said, "but then your birthday would be the worst ever." Sweet, sweet Jonah… "I know mom but I'd rather it be my worst day than your worst day…" Caleb chimed in, "I wish he could have lived long enough to open his Christmas presents. You know how he loved to open presents." Graci: "I wished he could have stayed for my birthday (next week) because I love him… she is really struggling in her mind with the "overness" of seeing Levi again (here). The other day she said, "Mom, I have tears because I want Levi" I said, "Me too Grace, I miss him sooo bad." Graci: "I want to go see him." Me: "Okay, maybe we'll go to the grave site tomorrow." Graci: "No, I want to see him when his eyes were closed." Sadness flooded my heart when it hit me that she was talking about him in the casket. I guess she knows that she can't see him alive but she'll settle with seeing him in the casket…sooo sad… as you can see, our conversations jump from bad to worse some days…

I am grateful for all we have learned through our tragedy. I still believe that Jesus is doing something way bigger than I can see. I still believe that His ways are better than ours which means Levi's death was best (which is really hard to say) . But my heart is still bleeding. I can step back and see a bit of the big picture but for the most part my daily life collides with that big picture and blows it out of the water. I miss him. I miss the simpler days. I even miss my naiveté, believing that I was completely safe from such a tragedy because my God would not allow that to happen to me. I was, in my mind, protected because surely the Lord knew that I could never survive such loss… I still choose to serve a God that I can't explain…*"To Him who is able to keep me from falling and to present me before His glorious presence without fault and with great joy."* (Jude 24).

~jami~

## August 24, 2002

On August 17th Graci turned 4 years old. She is officially a "big girl" now. We were crossing the street to go into the store and I put my hand down to hold hers. She looked up at me and said, "It's okay mom I'm 4 now, I'n (she gets her m's and n's mixed up) a big girl, I can cross the street all by myself." I am constantly amazed with her – well, with all my children. It's one of life's great mysteries to me that I am their mother and am supposed to be teaching them about life but there's no way that I could teach them more about life than they teach me every day... I took Graci to my mom's and then went to pick the boys up at school. As soon as they got in the car they said, "Where's Grace?" I said, "I took her to MaMa so that we could go get her a birthday present." You would have thought we were going to Disney World. They were totally psyched. But they were upset that they didn't know ahead of time so that they could have gotten their own money. I told them that I would pay for the gifts..."but mom, I want to buy her something from me. I know exactly what I'm gonna get her...I can't wait to see her face when she opens it..." My heart swelled with pride and joy as I listened to my 10 and 8 year old boys swim in excitement at the thought of giving. Little did they know they had given me a priceless gift before we ever made it to the store...Isn't that the way Abba (Daddy God) is? He gives us a wealth of knowledge and blessing in the children we step over every day. Sometimes when I see parents ignoring their children I want to say to them, "...Better listen up, you're missing the key to a treasure that you only have a certain window of time to open...if you're not careful you'll miss it, soon they'll be gone and the treasure will be forever lost."

Totally off the subject: I was talking to my Daddy the other day just remembering regrets I have in Levi's last days. But in talking about it I thought maybe it wasn't as bad as I thought... while Levi was in ICU there was an "incident" that I was ashamed of. Levi had just been extibated (breathing tube taken out) he was really struggling to breathe, turning a little blue even, there was fear in his eyes... there seemed to be no concern on the part of the doctors and nurses. Jeff, Lori and I kept going out to the nurses and saying, "there's a problem here, he's really struggling, could we get some help? (trying to be nice but wanting terribly to punch someone) every time, they would say, "we'll be in there in a minute." Well this happened about 4 times. It went on for about 20 minutes... I wanted to remain calm for Levi's sake. If he saw me panic then he would know something was really wrong. But it was too much for me. I lost it. I won't go into detail but it was not pretty, I went head long into panic mode, went out of the room talking VERY loudly to anyone who would listen...it was just a few seconds before every nurse and doctor within shouting distance was in our room... Levi was laying in bed with tubes running out of him, wide eyed watching the whole incident. I felt like a failure, I had lost control and made Levi feel even more afraid at the sight of me pointing and screaming at anyone who had ears...I wondered if he was ashamed of me. I have regretted that day for the better part of 9 months. But then the other day Caleb, Jonah, Graci and I were watching a show about a man fighting (literally) for his son to get treatment at a hospital that was denying him care for insurance reasons. Caleb looked up at me and said, "Would you do that for us?" I said, "Caleb there is no limit to what I would be willing to do for y'all... his face showed full satisfaction in that answer. It's like it gave him a deeper security in my love and devotion to him, a pride if you will. All of a sudden my mind went back to that day at the hospital. I thought for the first time. Maybe Levi was not ashamed of me for losing it. Maybe he saw something good. Maybe he saw me loving him the best way I could. Maybe he wasn't ashamed of me after all, maybe he was proud. Wow, that thought gave me relief. Oh Lord, May it be true that in that day that I saw as a failure he saw a mom that was willing to fight for him. I hope, I hope, I hope...

Lately, my heart has been packed full with thoughts and memories that are less than comfortable. Which has brought me to this place of "ponder". Lord, why is life so hard? Why is it that every person that has ever totally sold out to you has had a life packed with trials, failures, tragedy, pain???? Why does that happen? Why is it that the more answers I find about you the more questions I find as well? Why is it that the more You mold me into Your image and will, the more I see how far away from that goal I am?

When will I get to that place of comfort that I long for????? NEVER. My latest "lesson" is that comfort has nothing to do with walking with Christ. As a matter of fact if comfort is what I want I'd better "back out" now.

There was a letter found in the rubble of a Jewish ghetto in Poland after it was bombed by the Nazis. It was written by a child and it echoes my heart... "Lord, I do not ask you to make my life easy, I do ask you to make me strong."

And Jesus said, *"I tell you the truth, unless you change and become like little children, you will never enter the Kingdom of heaven."* Matthew 18:3

~jami~

**August 29, 2002**

A lot of people ask us how Caleb, Jonah and Graci are doing... so I thought I would give a little "sampler" of their hearts, how they're doing as of now. Basically this is a few conversations we've had in the last couple of days.

Yesterday Graci and I got in the car and were on our way to get the boys at school. All was well and we were having a pretty good day. But then I turned around and noticed Graci crying. I said, "What's wrong, Grace?" Rubbing her eyes, she said, "I miss Levi." So sad, so sweet. I stopped the car, got her out of her carseat and held her. We just hugged and cried together... "What do you miss doing with Levi the most? I asked (hoping I could get her mind off her sadness and on to some of their sweet memories.) "I just miss huggin' and kissin' him." What could I say except, "me too." We cried and hugged some more... later on, as we were getting close to the school she said, "I want to go to heaven." "Wow," I said, "me too but we have to wait our turn and it's not our turn until Jesus says so." "But I really want to go today, let's just drive there, we've been there before, let's go again..." At this point I was really confused..."We've never been to heaven..." It all came together in my mind when she said, "Yes we have, don't you remember when we went to see Levi with his eyes closed?" (…the night of the viewing/wake (whatever you call it), we told Graci that Levi was in heaven…we walked into the room with his casket and she saw him from across the room, looked up at us and said, "Is this heaven, because there's Levi.") Precious girl, there's so much that she doesn't understand, there's so much that I don't understand…

After we picked the boys up we were driving by the cemetery, I drove into the entrance, Caleb said, "Oh no mom, let's don't go in here, everyone starts crying." Jonah came back at him with, "Yeah but that's what family's for, we cry together." That was good enough for Caleb so we had our visit with Levi's sweet little body. (There's something so special about knowing that his body is close.)

I love how all the kids keep Levi in our day. Last night we were praying, focusing on being grateful for God's creation. This was Caleb's prayer: "Dear Father, thank you for your beautiful creation, thank you that you made the sky, the stars, the planets… and thank you that you made heaven for Levi to be in and someday we will be there too and when we get there we won't have to worry about anything else…" Jonah's prayer: "Lord, thank you for the world you made, thank you for the animals to love, thank you for the people to love…thank you that you gave us Levi to love and would you tell him that we love him and miss him right now, would you hug him for us? And of course Graci's prayer was a little simpler: "Dear Father, thank you for the ponies. In Jesus' name, amen."

Is that beautiful or what?

A few days ago I sensed that Caleb was a little down so we sat and chatted for a while. I just asked him how he was doing with Levi being gone. "Well, I miss him."

Then I asked how he feels toward God: "I don't know, what do you mean?"

Well, I said, "You know we prayed for Levi to be healed and he was but only for 3 weeks, and now he's gone…" Caleb, being a man of few words responded with, "Well I still love HIM."

I was reading through the boys journals (with their permission). I read them every once in a while just to check and see the condition of their hearts and to see how I need to pray for them. Here are a few excerpts:

JONAH'S:

"Levi was the bestest brother is the whole world. I love him so much he was so great. I love him so so so so much…I love you Levi.

"Levi was like a very best friend."

"Levi was so precious to me. I just love him so much."

"Dear Levi, I miss you so so so much, I am sorry if I was ever mean to you, I love you."

On each of these pages he has drawn pictures for Levi, sunshine, dogs, flowers, fish, birds, hearts…the things that Levi loved…

CALEB'S:

"I miss Levi, I wish I can be with him in heaven. I love Levi. I miss him. I want to be with him and hug him. I want to come home from school and see him and hug him, Why did Levi have to die?"

"Levi, I love you so much. So much that you cannot believe it. I love to hear you laugh. I love to watch cartoons with you. Football is fun to play with you too. You are good at football. We are a good team at baseball. We love sports don't we Levi? I love you Levi…"

Every time I read these I am blessed and I am broken. I am amazed at their new capacity to love. It is deeper, wider and more selfless than most adults I know… I have learned more about the person of Christ through my children in the last year and a half than in the prior 10 years of seeking Him. God is profoundly brilliant through them. He whispers to me through their words, He speaks to me through their prayers and He shouts to me through their painful tears. Teaching me, showing me that just when I think I know all the dimensions of my Savior's personality there is still more to be known and loved of Him. Tim Hansel wrote: "While one great tragedy of the world is that many people are unfamiliar with Jesus, it is equally tragic that some of us are too familiar with Him, in the sense that 'we think we know, we think we really understand' the full significance of His life within us and among us." With that in mind I think HE is saving me from the "tragedy" of familiarity by way of the tragedy of Levi's death. Does that make sense?

I guess what I'm saying can be summed up in and through this story: It was the middle of World War 2. Men were giving their best on the front lines. Somehow one of them scrounged up an old beaten-up phonograph and a record. the record was of none other than Enrico Caruso, considered at that time the greatest singer in the world.

That evening as they sat around the tent listening to the scratchy, rather worn record on a weathered phonograph, there were two distinct groups of listeners. Some heard only the scratches on the record. Others, who listened more deeply, heard the "master's" voice…

Our lives have been very confusing, scratchy and unclear. But we are starting to hear the message of THE MASTER that is coming through loud and clear but only if we have ears to hear it.

~jami~

## September 8, 2002

Graci and I were singing the song "My favorite things" from the movie "The Sound of Music" but I couldn't remember all the words so I went looking for the video which I hadn't seen for a while – which meant it must be in the storage room in the basement. I ventured into the less traveled room.   I entered hesitantly, not only because it's such a mess but also because Levi's medical paraphernalia is in there.  His MRI's, his old oxygen mask, syringes, medical tape, saline to flush his broviac, medicines... the bag/backpack that I used to take everywhere we went that had everything we could possibly need... everything except a cure...

I didn't find the video but I did see all the "Levi stuff." I was going to just look at it and walk out quickly but I didn't. I couldn't. I walked toward it. I started rummaging through all the memories that go with it. My mind was overcome with mental pictures of the "life" before. Just for "old time sake" I put on a sanitary mask and picked up a syringe. How familiar it was. How comforting... I wondered if I could still remember the "process" that I knew so well... I screwed a sanitary needle onto the syringe, I got a bottle of saline, pushed air into it and then watched as the saline flooded into the syringe, 10cc's, pushing the extra air out and unscrewing the needle to attach it to his broviac and flush it... but there is no Levi at the other end of the broviac, there is no broviac... I imagined him choosing who would be the "lucky one" (he used to pick which one of the kids got to push the fluid in once I had set it up.) He always loved to see the excitement on the face of the "chosen one".... I miss those days. I miss the responsibility, I miss him...

Graci and I met Jeff for breakfast at the Cracker Barrel. We were sitting on the front porch waiting for him. I was in a big rocking chair and she, of course, had chosen a small white rocking chair right next to me. We were just talking and rocking. Then she looked past me at the rocking chair on my other side. It was another chair identical to her little one. She got up out of her chair and walked to the empty chair... she pushed it and made it rock back and forth, back and forth. I just watched, wondering what she was doing. Then she looked at me and said, "I'm pretending Levi is in this chair." I smiled and said, "he used to love this place didn't he?" "yes ma'am, and I wish he was here..." She let go of the chair and went back to hers. We were just quiet together but I watched out of the corner of my eye as "Levi's chair" rocked slower and slower until it was completely still. The stillness and emptiness of it suddenly became painfully loud to me... to us both.

I am beginning to see that there is a part of me that will be forever sad. There will be a "sigh" forever inside of me too deep for words. I've heard some people say: "Oh you'll heal, you'll be fine, someday you won't be so sad." Well, I know that I'm a novice at this. But I have come to the conclusion that I will never not have a sad place, a longing to be with Levi, an amputation of sorts. But I am learning to live in it. I am learning that it is that very "missing piece" that keeps my heart and mind fixed on eternal things. It's the "empty rocking chair" that makes me get up and live life more fully for Christ. I am sad. Truly, truly more sad than I ever thought possible. But when I am joyful I am more joyful than I ever thought possible (even though the joyful bursts are few and far between) .

I guess what I'm trying to say is: Being sad is okay. Being dissatisfied with this world and all its "bummers" is even a good thing because I have a tighter grip on the fact that we were not made for this world, therefore it is increasingly lacking what we need and that is hard to live in... but it is true. Jeff and I were talking today. He had gone to the bookstore and ended up talking to a Buddhist monk. Jeff basically witnessed to this guy for about thirty minutes telling him about the person of Christ and how we were created to worship Him, to have a personal relationship with Him... he called me afterwards and said, "Oh Jami, while I was talking to that guy I felt so close to the Lord. All I want to do is share HIM with lost people"... "I guess that's why people who are martyred for Christ find it easy to "let go" of this world. They're satisfied. They have done what they were created to do and they can "go" in the peace of knowing they've fought the good fight and kept the faith...

...that sounds so spiritually "in control" ...and when I read over it I even sense strength, which makes me want to erase it because that's not what's going on in me. I am weak, confused and all cluttered up inside. I just know that HIS plan is good in the end no matter how it may appear today.

I say along with Thoman Merton, "My Lord God, I have no idea where I am going. I do not see the road ahead of me. I cannot know for certain where it will end. Nor do I really know myself, and the fact that I think I am following your will does not mean that I am actually doing so. But I believe that the desire to please You does in fact please You. "

"I have found that the most extravagant dreams of boyhood have not surpassed the great experience of being in the will of God, and I believe that nothing could be better."
Jim Elliott (Martyr for Christ)

fumbling victoriously,

~jami~


## September 21, 2002

It's 4:45 am. Jeff just left for the airport. It's pouring down rain and I can't sleep. After he walked out the door I ran to our bedroom window and watched him drive away. I felt afraid... "Lord, please bring him back to me..." It's funny, I used to live in this bubble of "that would never happen..." but now my bubble is gone and I realize that anything can happen. It's a scary place. Knowing the way things are in this world we had to take time to talk about "what if" before he left. We went over insurance, money... and then we went over, what he would tell Levi if he got to heaven before me... strange thing to let my heart and mind go there. In my mind I saw this picture of Jeff and Levi running to each other, hugging, kissing and knowing each other again, knowing love without being bound to words to express it. I still see that snapshot in my mind... all of this made me think of all the special moments, mental snapshots that I have stored up in my mind. I scroll through them and I see a plethora of sweet things.

There's the day I walked down the isle to marry Jeff, our whole life ahead of us. I see the first time I laid eyes on each one of my children after giving birth to them. The wonder of it all, the desire to stop all time long enough to grasp the vastness of the blessing. But no, time kept moving, going, going... then I "go" to the days when I had 4 children under 6, wondering if I would ever make it through the day in and day out of it all, yet knowing that someday this time in my life would be something I would long to go back to. Wow, my mind is wide open now, so many moments I would have just stopped to hold on to if only I could have. The time I prayed with my brother, David to receive Christ in the back of his truck at Stone Mountain Park (after praying for 15 years). The first time I saw Dicky (my other brother) hold his newborn baby. The time that Lori and Levi were sitting on my couch just looking at each other, staring, trying desperately to stop time from bringing what we all knew was coming...the time I looked up from praying over Levi and saw my mom and dad holding on to each other and me, crying out to God, a hard moment but beautiful, so beautiful was the sight of our families coming together so passionately. Such fleeting moments. I want them back. I don't like how time keeps rolling by waiting for no one. No matter how hard I may try to hold on to life it is always slipping away. It's not mine, it can't be kept, saved or stored up...

Jeff's life verse is Acts 20:24, *"However I consider my life worth nothing to me if only I may finish the race and complete the task the Lord Jesus has given me. The task of testifying to the gospel of God's grace."* And there you have it!! If we consider this life nothing in light of what Christ has done for us we can live knowing that in the end HE will capture all our "moments" and He will hold them tightly for us so that when we stand before Him having been faithful all the way, we will find our treasures stored up. They will finally be ours to keep. Time will not bind us, the enemy will no longer chase us. Our moments will no longer flee. That is sooo worth waiting for.

Please pray for Jeff as he is in Alaska on a mission trip. Please pray for him safety, peace and a deeper walk with Jesus.

Love to you all,

~jami~

## October 3, 2002

It's October now, that time of year when you anticipate the holidays, the weather is changing, pumpkins are everywhere... I remember last year whenever we'd see the pumpkins Levi would get so excited because it meant his birthday was right around the corner (November 13th). He'd say, "I see pumpkins, you know what that means???" His eyes excited about the soon coming day. I'm dreading that day this year...I remember his last birthday...We went over to my mom and dad's house (it wasn't finished being built yet) we stood around in the unfurnished den eating cake and ice cream. He couldn't stand but he sat in his wheelchair as the rest of us danced to some of his favorite songs. He found such pleasure in watching the rest of us being silly. I think we all knew that our days were numbered so there was an unspoken sadness but we all tried to keep our heads up for his sake. I can see him in my mind, so swollen and uncomfortable looking... I wonder if he knew. I wonder if the Lord had given him some idea of what was to come. It was only 4 days later that we found ourselves at Egleston in ICU. What hard days those were but I would go back there if I could. Beggars can't be choosers, I'd take a bad days over no days.

Last weekend was such a busy time for me. I was surrounded by people the whole weekend.

I can only take so much "smothered" time, I am so in need of "alone" time now. I have to take time to remember, to cry, to be sad and not feel like I have to "be all together." When I'm around a lot of people I feel like I have a huge secret, even kinda like I'm lying. I'm walking and talking, I'm smiling, laughing… but inside I'm dying. Surrounded by people yet so lonely for my used to be life. When people ask, "So, how are you?" I want so much to be able to say how badly I hurt without falling apart." But the general population isn't ready for that, for me when I'm totally real.

It's funny how I go from feeling victorious to complete defeat so quickly. Just last week I was feeling like the Lord was bringing healing to me. Today I feel as if it was just yesterday that Levi left. When I walk past his pictures my eyes automatically divert, I can't look (Sometimes I make myself stare at his sweet face until my eyes are too filled with tears to see him anymore.) It hurts so bad…oh to feel my arms hold him again… to touch his face…to give him baths and hear his whiny little voice as he came down the steps in the mornings… to hear Caleb, Jonah and Graci come in from playing in the cul-de-sac to check on him, just to hear them say his name…"Levi" I love to hear his name spoken out loud. How can a heart desire something so deeply that it knows it will never have again (until heaven)? Some days I am drowning in a sea of sorrow. There is no relief. Other days I walk in joy and hopefulness. I've found that the only time that I feel a reprieve from the sadness is when I am talking about what the Lord has done in the hearts of my family and friends (and my own heart). That sounds really…"on top"… but it's not really, it's a discovery type thing, every day I live without Levi I see something of the "bigger plan." That in no way means that the sadness and longing for Levi are gone. It just means that I see it, I don't feel it. Rita Springer sings a song that says: "I don't understand Your ways but I will give you my song and I'll give you all of my praise. You hold on to all of my pain and with it you are pulling me closer, pulling me into your ways… Now around every corner and up every mountain I'm not looking for crowns anymore or the water from fountains I'm desperate in seeking…frantic, believing the sight of your face is all that I'm needing… I will say to you: 'Oh it's gonna be worth it, It's gonna be worth it all…'" Man how that speaks to me. I am so frustrated with my restlessness with this world. I'm caught somewhere in the middle of loving life and hating it, hoping for the future and not wanting to go any further than today, tomorrow seems too far ahead…( I don't know where I'm going with all this rambling…I only know that I miss Levi. I miss him so bad today. I have his picture right here next to me, I look at it and hurt so badly wanting it to be more than just a piece of paper. )

I believe HIS promises. I believe it's all gonna be worth it someday, I do, I do, I do…It's today I'm having a hard time with…And the holidays, his birthday, my birthday…Oh Lord, how? How will we make it????

My brother told me that he heard (in the grieving circle) that the 9th month is the place where most people "hit the wall." Well, it's been 9 months and I've got "brick in my face." I feel like I'm at ground zero, day 1…

Jesus said, "Blessed is he who is not offended by me." I am trying so hard, praying desperately that my flesh and pain will not be offended by this "plan" that I live in. I guess that is something that I will fight for the rest of my life. I will press on pursuing The One who knows me, loves me and will meet all my needs. I am truly "frantic, believing the sight of HIS face is all that I'm needing."

{Please pray for us, we have so many changes ahead of us, we're longing for change but afraid of it at the same time. Holy Spirit go with us… stay with us… be with us… We can't, we won't move or breathe without your presence…}

Thank you,

~jami~


## October 18, 2002

It's mid October and Jeff and I are restless. We are in need of change but must wait for God's timing. We have our house for sale but the market is really slow. Sometimes I think I can't live in this house with all its painful memories another day…other times I think I could never leave this house and all its beautiful memories… which way do I go?? I'm stuck in the middle of ashes and beauty…strange place…

I am missing Levi so desperately, as always of course but I'm in a "wave" of missing him beyond the usual daily sadness. I think of the fact that I lived 31 years without him. I only had five years with him but those five years drastically changed who I am. That's amazing to me. What love I have for him. It has only gotten stronger since he left. I still have such passionate, undying, committed love toward him. The only thing different is that I have no way to act on it…how desperately I want to "do" something for him. How I would love to lavish my love on him in some way one more time. I love my other children no less than I love Levi but I still have the privilege of showing them on a daily basis. I have learned their "love languages" and try to remember to "speak" love to them in their own "words." Levi's love language was just being with him. To sit on the couch and watch a cartoon with him was like flowers and candy to me. To lay down in front of the fireplace and snuggle was one of his favorite things. If I reached over to him, pulled up his shirt and scratched his back he would melt beneath my hands. Showing love was simple with him. It didn't cost anything… I'm remembering (once again) laying in the hospital bed with him…he was paralyzed except his right hand…he reached over to scratch my back even though it took most of the strength he had. It means more now that I'm remembering that back scratching spoke such love to him…he was saying he loved me in his own "words." Sweet, sweet little man of mine. How I miss you Levi, I wish you could talk to me…I wish I could show you my love again…

Oh Lord, while you are with Levi this very moment would you scratch his sweet little back? Tell him it's what I wish I could do for him and it will speak from the deepest places in my heart…in his language.

…seeing him in my mind makes me think again of the verse in when David's son died and he was absolutely devastated… he came to grips with the fact that his son was gone and said *"… I shall go to him, but he shall not return to me."* (2 Samuel 12:23). They're together. I'm sure it seemed like forever that they had to wait but the wait is over for them now. I'm happy for them…

# Levi's Legacy

In my longing to be reunited with Levi I question myself, "Do I long for the blessing (Levi) more than the blesser (Jesus)? So, my feeble prayer is "Lord, help my heart to long to see your face, to show you love through obedience, to run this race even though it has turned out to be harder than I had once thought it would be."

I don't know where I am right now with the Lord. I'm kinda in the dark but I just gotta keep moving toward HIM. Martin Luther King Jr. said, "If you can't fly, run. If you can't run, walk. If you can't walk, crawl, but by all means keep moving." I guess you'd say I'm crawling, but learning, growing… I guess it's really a good place (not a feel good place) but a good place just the same. It's good because I think I'm doing what I'm supposed to do, getting to know the character of God, discovering something of Him that I knew nothing of before. "It's during the tough times much more than the good times that I am growing into the creature He intended. Therefore the cries of my heart that come from my spiritual desert are those that possibly please Him the most… He wants me to learn to walk and therefore must remove His hand; and if my will to walk is there He is pleased even with my stumbles, falls and temporary crawls. Surely He is most pleased when we, His children no longer desire to run this race but still intend to do His will, look around a universe from which every trace of Him seems to have vanished, and ask 'why have You forsaken me' and still obey" (C.S. Lewis, Screwtape Letters).

In the words of psychiatrist Gerald May, "In reality, our lack of fulfillment is the most precious gift we have. It is the source of our passion, our creativity, our search for God. All the best of life comes out of our human yearning — not our being satisfied." Therefore, I am striving to be grateful not for the pain itself but for the opportunity to respond, by mining good out of what looks (and is) really, really bad. {Phillip Yancey}

fumbling victoriously,

~jami~


## November 11, 2002

It's the end of a busy weekend. Tomorrow begins the week of Levi's first birthday in heaven! How happy I am for him. I know that every day (even though heaven is not bound by time) is probably like a birthday there. Caleb and I were talking about heaven and what it might be like (even though our imaginations could never come close but we gave it a shot anyway). He came to the conclusion that Heaven has the constant feeling of "just about Christmas." Surely that warm fuzzy feeling is a tiny foretaste of things to come. The great thing about heaven I imagine, is that there is no "morning after" when the anticipation is over and the normal routine must resume…

My niece, Sydney and Levi were born two days apart. For all their lives we celebrated their birthdays together. They shared birthday cakes, candles, balloons… they never knew any different it was just the way it was. This year will be new. How my heart longs for the same old thing. I wonder if Syd will feel "short changed" this year because she doesn't get to share her day with him.

# Levi's Legacy

Wednesday is Levi's birthday. We're all going to the cemetery. The kids are going to write everything they wish they could say to Levi on helium balloons and then we're going to let them go. They are very aware of the fact that those balloons will not actually make it to heaven but it will be a tiny way to express their love... (I'll be sending one too)

A helium balloon goes with the wind, it is weak and so small in the backdrop of the sky... just like the words I use to express the sadness I feel without Levi here. I try so hard to paint pictures of how I am feeling, what is happening inside me... but they are so small in the backdrop of my broken heart. I was just thinking about how to describe love. How do you? How could you possibly put words to what happens inside you when you see your newborn baby for the first time (I remember thinking, "I can't believe I had anything to do with this miracle.") or how your heart swells when you see your baby laugh for the first time, blow kisses, wave, say "I love you", walk, run...? There's no way!!! Likewise there's no way to express the depth of the hole inside me now. The backwardness of "sweet November" coming without him here to celebrate it with us. I know that some people think that we should be about ready to get back to the usual routine. NEVER! We are not the same, we will never be the same. And that's that!!! This is the way I look at it: God is good, He is in full control, He is and was not surprised by that brain tumor and Levi's death. And if I believe that I must believe that Levi was never intended to live past December 20th 2001. God had strong intentions in Levi's death and its timing. To go back to things the way we were would be to spit in God's face. He meant for it to rock our world, for us to think more eternally, to live more recklessly abandoned to His ways, wherever they may take us... I want to get all that HE intended for us in this heartbreak. "The grapes must be crushed to become wine" and we have truly been crushed, to go back to a "grape" just will not do. To do so would dishonor God and undercut the depth of love we have for Levi. I like that verse in Ephesians 5:15; it works well in my heart, *"Be very careful, then, how you live – not as unwise but as wise, making the most of every opportunity... sing and make music in your heart to the Lord, always giving thanks to God the Father for everything, in the name of our Lord Jesus Christ."*(vs. 19) I want to be careful, very, very careful how I live now. Everything is different now, as it should be. There are some good things that HE is doing in me now. I am less likely to sweat the small stuff, I love more deeply, I have a deeper "place" for people who are hurting. I waste less time being busy and use more time being still. I don't rush, rush, rush to be what other people think I should be, I'd rather stay home, curl up on the couch with my children and touch them, hold them, scratch backs because I can for today, tomorrow they might not be here... I have a really cool thing going on inside me these days too: I want to know God, the real God. Not a "churchy" God. Not the God I used to know because after the last 10 months of searching for Him and the truth of His character I have discovered that everything I thought of him was a "shortshot." I feel as if I am at the beginning of a really great adventure. HE is a treasure just waiting to be discovered but like all hidden treasure it must be wanted, it can't be stumbled upon...

Jeff's great uncle, Herb Paynter Sr. has been sick and in the hospital for the last three or four days, he's 88 years old. An incredible man of God. His life is one of the finest examples of "finishing well" I've ever seen. We were at the hospital visiting and he prayed for me. He could hardly talk but he prayed for me… He knew I was speaking at a Christmas tea in December. He was so excited that I would be speaking to people that don't know Jesus. At the end of his prayer he said something like this: "Lord, I can't wait to see what You do through jami… I know I probably won't be here but I'm sure I'll hear about it in Heaven." He was right! He went to be with his Lord today (November 11th, Sydney's birthday) at 10:15am. What an incredible entrance that must have been… He spent his allotted 88 years well, very, very well… all the way to the end and now he can really say, *"I fought the good fight, I finished the race, I kept the faith. Now there is in store for me the crown of righteousness, which the Lord, the righteous Judge, will award to me…"* 2 Timothy 4:7, 8. Oh the joy he must be experiencing… I wonder if he's seen Levi yet…

**November 13, 2002**

Well, it's here, it's Levi's birthday. It's not even 7:00 am yet and it's already hard. I guess my mom and dad won't be calling to sing their usual song like they do for all the grandchildren on their birthdays. I miss that… I'm downstairs in the basement at my desk all alone in the silence. Usually on a birthday the morning silence is broken early because the birthday boy or girl can't sleep from the excitement of the special day ahead… I can see him in my mind coming down those stairs with his hair sticking up, his face all puffy from sleep, rubbing his eyes then putting his arms up to be held… after I have him in my arms he lays his head on my shoulder about to fall asleep but then remembers to say, "I want pancakes please" then his head falls back to my shoulder…I wonder if there are pancakes in heaven? He really liked blueberry pancakes…I'm sure when they are served he will cheer like he always did here and then say, "thanks mom, you're the best!!"

Today at his birthday party I want it to be a joyful time but I'm afraid. I can hardly drive into that cemetery without bawling, how will I make it through a party. How will I listen the all the kids as they say what they wish they could say to Levi and then release a balloon then watch the balloon go farther and farther away, until it disappears into the clouds, just like Levi did. It doesn't sound like I'm happy that Levi is celebrating his first birthday in heaven does it? I really am! I guess I feel a little left out and wish I could hug him. I know that Jesus is doing way better on the whole birthday thing than I ever could but I really want to be a bigger part of his special day. My heart is confused… I say along with Virginia Bell (Ruth Bell Graham's mother) when walking from the place her 10 month old son was just buried, "I have a song in my heart but I can't keep the tears from my eyes."

10:20 am – I was on the treadmill running as hard as I could. I guess I was trying to get away from my aching heart. While I was running I was listening to a worship CD I haven't listened to since Levi's funeral day. (Caleb had asked if we could listen to it today) So, I got it out (Phillips, Craig and Dean, Worship, If you don't have it, you need it:)) … I was listening, running, crying…crying sooo hard…It was a different kind of crying though. I can't describe what it was like, I guess it was hopeful. It started as I was listening to the words of this song: "I don't know how to say exactly how I feel, I can't begin to tell you what your love has meant to me. I'm lost for words. Is there a way to show the passion in my heart? Can I express how truly great I think you are, my dearest friend? Lord this is my desire to pour my love on you, like oil upon your feet, like wine for you to drink like water from my heart, I pour my love on you, If praise is like perfume I lavish mine on you till every drop is gone, I pour my love on you." – In my heart I was doing just that, at the feet of Jesus. I saw myself as the woman who poured out her most expensive perfume (after all, my children are the most valuable things I have) onto His feet... I saw his feet in my mind, I touched them...remembering how often I used to rub Levi's feet with oil...it dawned on me that when I "lavish" my love on Jesus, I mean really, really love on Him...I get to do that to Levi,again. I could almost feel his little chubby feet in my hands. Thank you Jesus for letting me touch Levi when my heart goes for YOU. How great YOU are, how small I am, how awesome is your mighty hand,,, I am captured by the wonder of it all...

11:00am – Graci is missing Levi so bad: "Mom, I wish Levi were here. I want to read my Pooh, book with him..."

11:30am – Caleb and Jonah have a big fight. They've been frustrated all morning... I call them into my room to talk about it...they apologized to each other. Then we talked about how important it is to forgive. Then I made them hug, they shyly complied. Then I told them to kiss on the cheek, they were shocked that I would ask them to kiss each other (since they're big now). I said, "you know why I'm gonna make you kiss?" "why?" "Because you have each other, don't you wish you could kiss Levi? you can't but you can kiss the ones you have for now." What a great "grown up thing" to know at such a young age (what an advantage they have). I told them if they got into another fight I'd make them kiss on the lips :) ... they got along great the rest of the day.

2:30pm – We arrived at the cemetery. I felt okay (surprisingly). The whole family was there. We (all 15 of us) had helium balloons, we wrote what we wish we could say to Levi, we held them and on the count of 3 we yelled as loud as we could "WE LOVE YOU LEVI !!!" then we let the balloons go and watched them disappear into the clouds...What a sweet moment. I hope that somehow he saw from paradise that we have not and will not EVER forget...

5:00pm – We had a big dinner together, sang happy birthday to Levi and blew out the candles. (It was a Spongebob cake)

After that we just hung out. Truly the Lord has been good to carry us, once again.

Today I have a grateful heart. I didn't think I would feel this way. I thought this day might be a breeding ground for self pity. But the Lord has shown me all that I have today. I have a family that stopped everything and drove long distances to be with us, to help us, to "enter in", to love us... How grateful I am. I didn't think I could feel this way again. But I do, stronger than before. I came across this story today and it describes who I hope I become someday:

She had some kind of "wasting disease," her different powers fading away over the march of the month. A student happened upon her on a coincidental visit. The student kept going back, drawn by the strange force of the woman's joy.

Though she could no longer move her arms and legs, she would say, "I'm just so happy I can move my neck." When she could no longer move her neck, she would say, "I'm just so glad I can hear and see."

When the young student finally asked the old woman what would happen if she lost her sound and sight, the gentle old lady said, "I'll just be so grateful that you come to visit."

Is there any freedom like that of a grateful heart??? I have a long way to go but the goal for me is to open my eyes and see the vast landscape of all I have been given. Surely the great enemy, which is fear of loss, will be disarmed on that day.

G.K. Chesterton made an interesting remark that I really like. He said, "The worst moment for an atheist is when he/she feels grateful and there is no one to thank." How grateful I am that He has revealed to me to whom I am to be grateful :) :) :) :)

~jami~

# It continues…

This journey has not ended. As a matter of fact I think it has only just begun. I see that my life is (as scripture says) a race to be run and all my heartbreak has purpose. I know that as a follower of Christ I am only to expect more but I consider that our present sufferings are not worth comparing with the glory that will be revealed in us. Romans 8:18

I pray that this record of HIS great faithfulness will deepen your love for Him… that the journey of your own heart will press on, deeper into His truth and goodness… May you be a slave to His freedom and may you finish well.

~jami~